How to Draw
NeoPopRealism
ADVANCED
abstract IMAGES

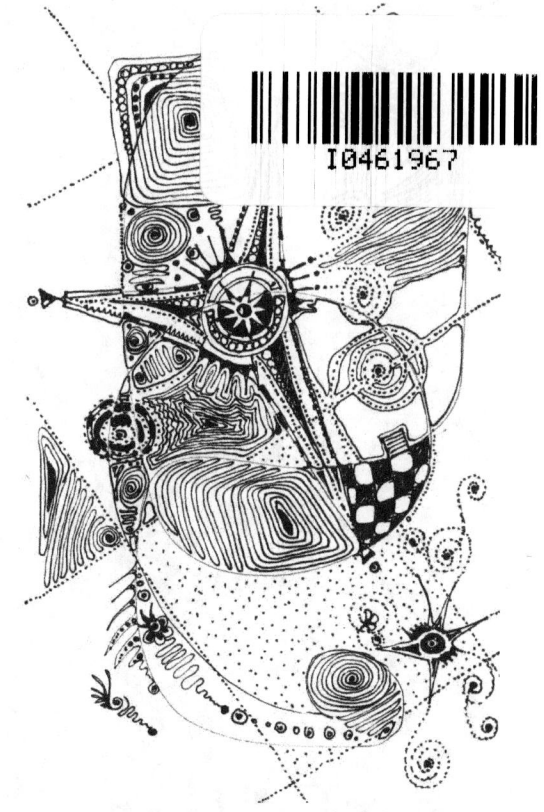

Ink Backgrounds
NeoPopRealism PRESS
ILLUSTRATED BY **NADIA RUSS**

2

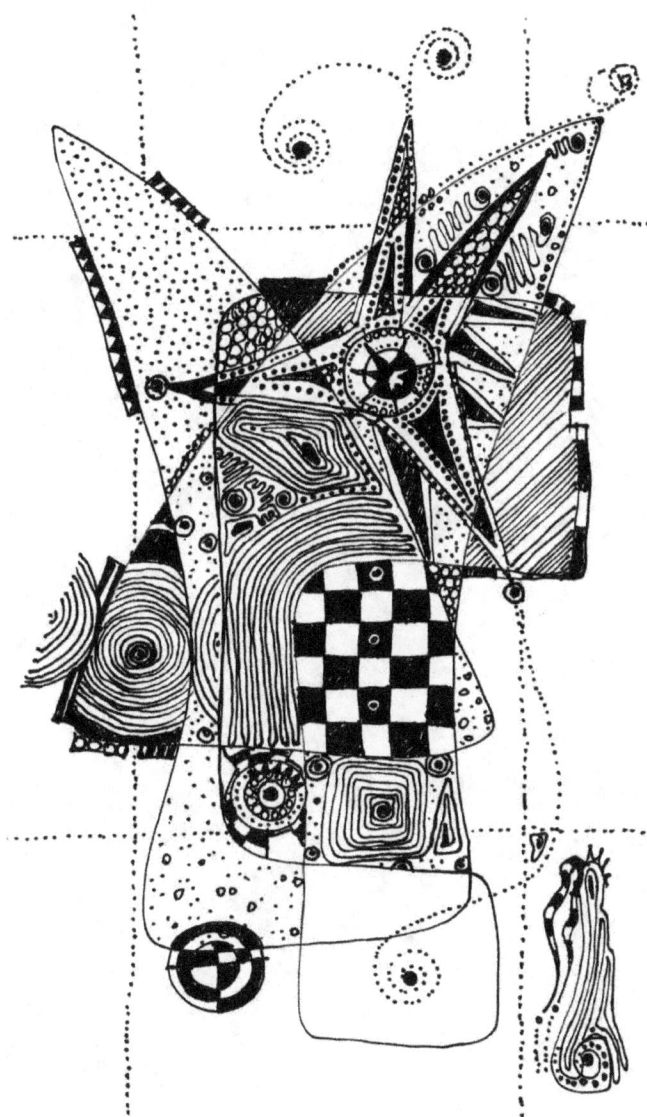

Abstract A, ink on paper

NeoPopRealist abstract backgrounds are whimsical; they are simple and complicated at the same time and require imagination and artistic intuition to create the balanced compositions. When you draw the NeoPopRealist backgrounds you develop your sense of harmony.

How to Draw

NeoPopRealism

ADVANCED
abstract IMAGES

Ink Backgrounds

NeoPopRealism PRESS
ILLUSTRATED BY **NADIA RUSS**

First time published in 2012 by NeoPopRealism PRESS
PO BOX 366
New York, NY 10013

NeoPopRealismPRESS@mail.com

How to Draw NeoPopRealism Advanced Abstract Images: Ink Backgrounds

© Copyrighted in 2012 by Nadia Russ

ISBN-13: 978-0615592558
ISBN-10: 0615592554

12 13 14 15 16   10 9 8 7 6 5 4 3 2 1

Published in the United States of America
Language: English

This book teaches how to draw NeoPopRealism advanced abstract images / ink backgrounds.

For teenagers and adults.

Author: Nadia Russ
Illustrated by Nadia Russ

www.neopoprealism.org

CONTENT

INTRODUCTION

The NeoPopRealism ink drawing concept was created by Nadia Russ in 1989. It was an experiment. She was trying to connect to the Universe and let the Universe use her as a Conductor when she created her drawings. She didn't want to follow any other artists' achievements, she decided to create absolutely new art style, like Picasso (Cubism), Dali (Surrealism), Andy Warhol (Pop Art) and a few other worldwide known artists had done.

Nadia Russ took her ink pen and began to draw a flowing line that turned into shapes, figures, often faces. Then, some sections (or all), that appeared, she filled with different repetitive patterns. She never used eraser because if a mistake made, it disappears with the following repetitive patterns, which also balance the whole composition. Her work was unique; no one did anything like this before.

Later, January 4, 2003, Nadia Russ created a word NeoPopRealism and internationally announced the new style of visual arts.

8

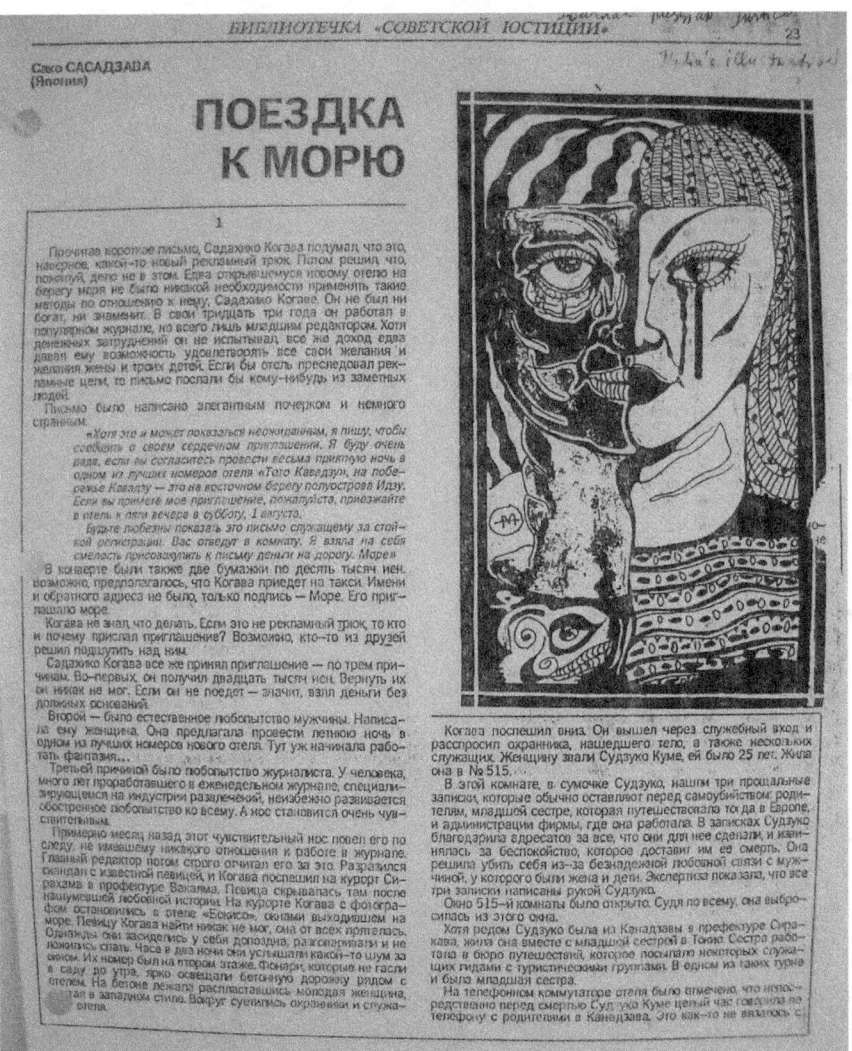

Nadia Russ illustrated a story by Saho Sasadzava for the *Russian Justice* Journal, 1992, Moscow, Russia

Get inspired

W hen you focus on success, you fall into the trap of comparing yourself to others, feeling envious. Instead, focus on getting better every day, focus on excellence. Men perceive, have emotions, thoughts, sensations, purposes, and desires. Gratitude floods your body and brain with emotions that uplift and energize you. Use your strengths for a bigger purpose beyond yourself. Focus on what you are giving instead of what you are getting, it makes every your step more rewarding and meaningful. . .

Your artwork is reflection of you, your moods; also it depends on what your artistic tasks are. Some of your NeoPopRealism work can have light backgrounds, but other - very busy, with complicated-looking, whimsical ornaments, where line twists and turns seemed unpredictably. The drawing of the busy abstracts/backgrounds is meditative process. Meditative state of mind is the highest state in which our mind can exists. When you are drawing your whimsical ornaments, your mind is open for the renewal. And more you draw, more relaxed you are. The repetitive patterns' drawing process invites you to the world where everything is simple as the sun and sky, and you are mesmerized by this simplicity and by the drawing process itself. After you finish one pattern, you begin draw anther, and so on. The images look complicated, but sometimes not all are that complicated when you start execute them. Concept is: *Line creates sections; sections fill with the repetitive patterns, using ink pen. You never use eraser.* With this drawing method you can achieve not only the interesting artistic results, but also the purity of your mind. Use your imagination. It is like a journey to the world of unknown with good feeling, knowing that you can turn the complexity into simplicity. This drawing is intuitive. Believe in yourself: you are a magician who can execute magic with the ink pen. You need no eraser because if a 'mistake' happened, it disappears with the following repetitive patterns that balance the whole composition. Isn't that magic?

Get your black ink pen *Foray Rolle Rollerball Medium 0.7 mm*, *Sharpie* or any similar pen and a piece of cardstock paper 8.5"x11" sold in Office Depot and other stores. Cut paper into two pieces, 5.5"x8.5" each. You will need one piece. In future, you can use ink pen - thin or thick - and type and size of paper depending on your artistic tasks. For your first drawings you can use pages of this book.

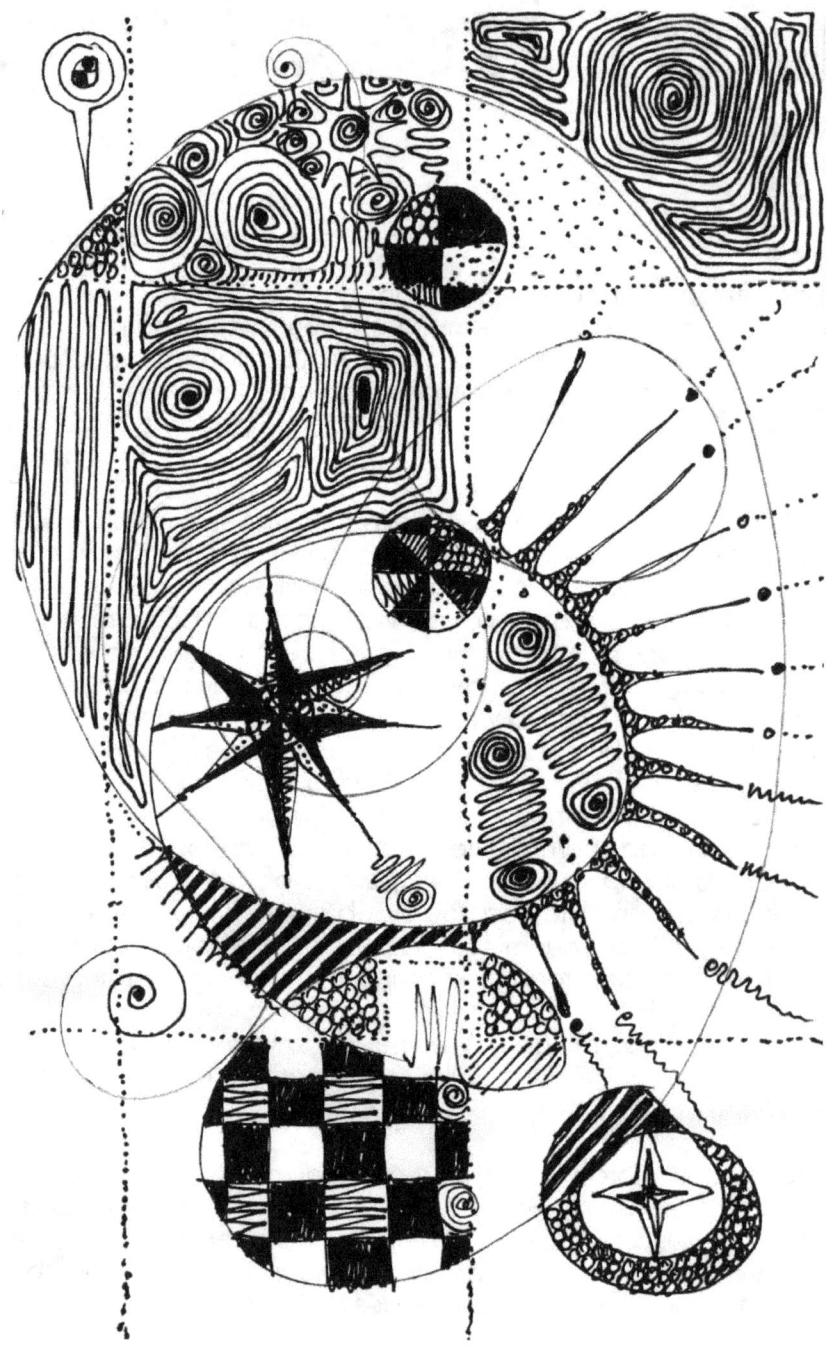

Abstract B, ink on paper

How to create NeoPopRealist Abstract C

The following pages will show you step-by-step how to create advanced abstract background for NeoPopRealism ink artwork that contains faces, figures or other objects. Also you can use such abstracts as the independent graphic designs. You need an imagination and particular artistic skills to draw this abstract. Every following picture includes new detail(s). The complete image looks like this:

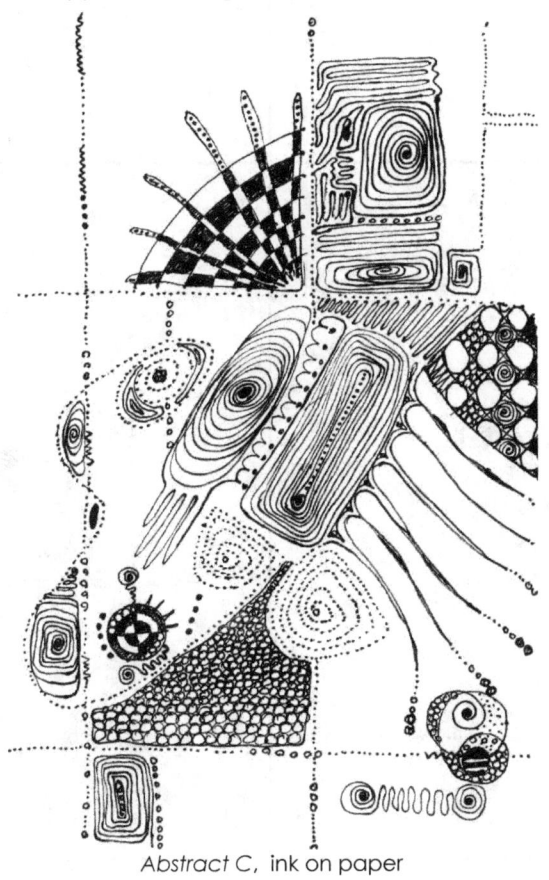

Abstract C, ink on paper

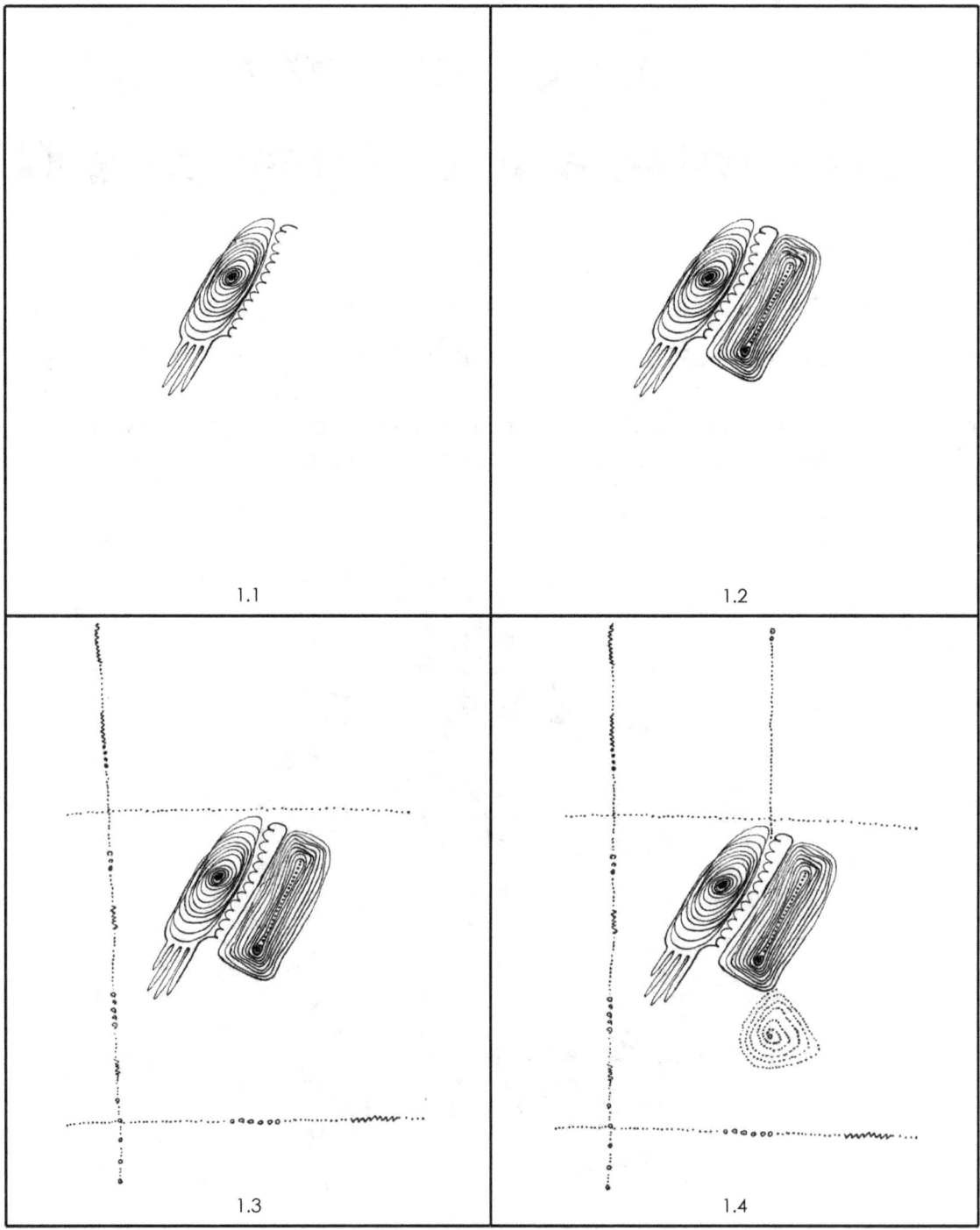

1.1

1.2

1.3

1.4

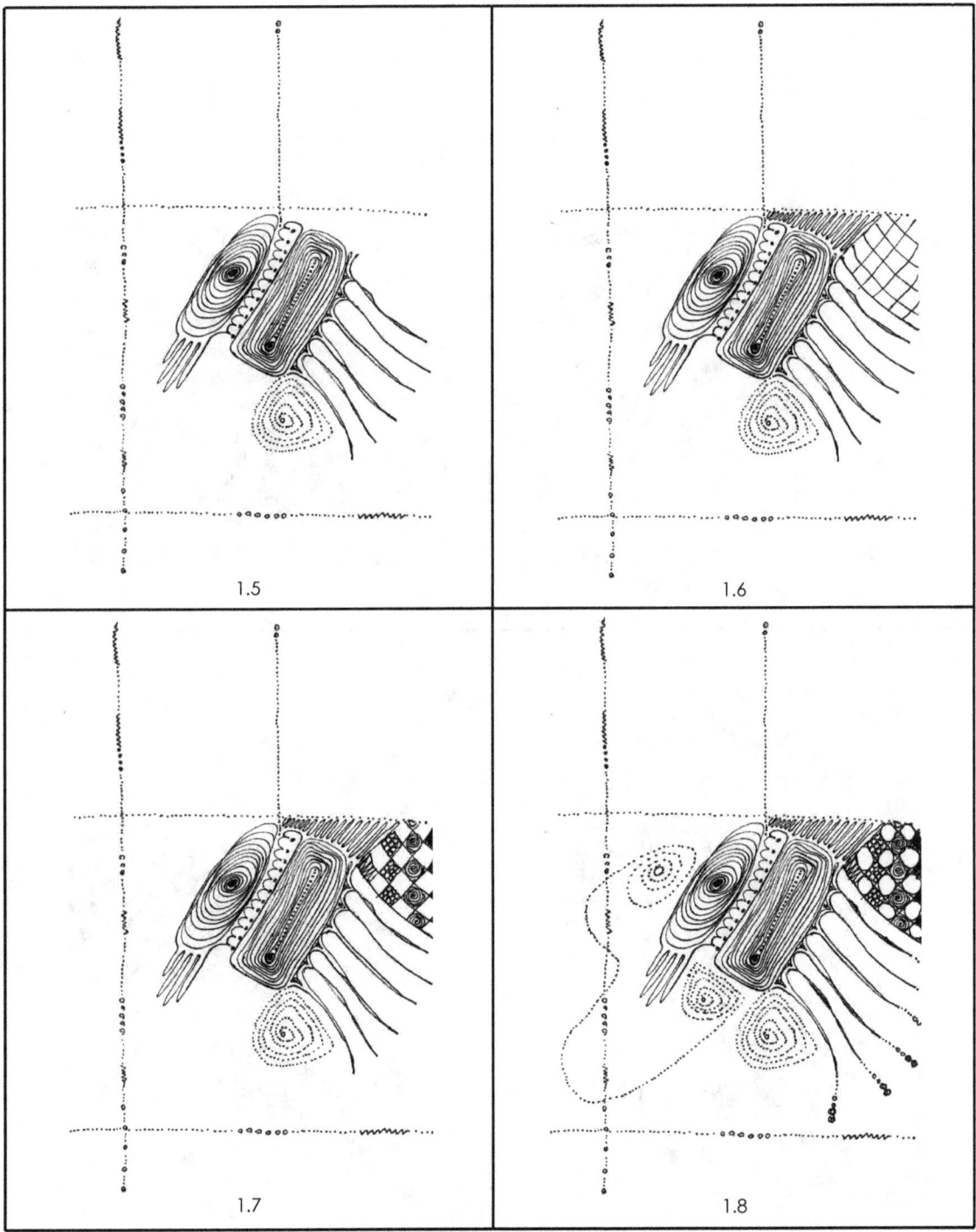

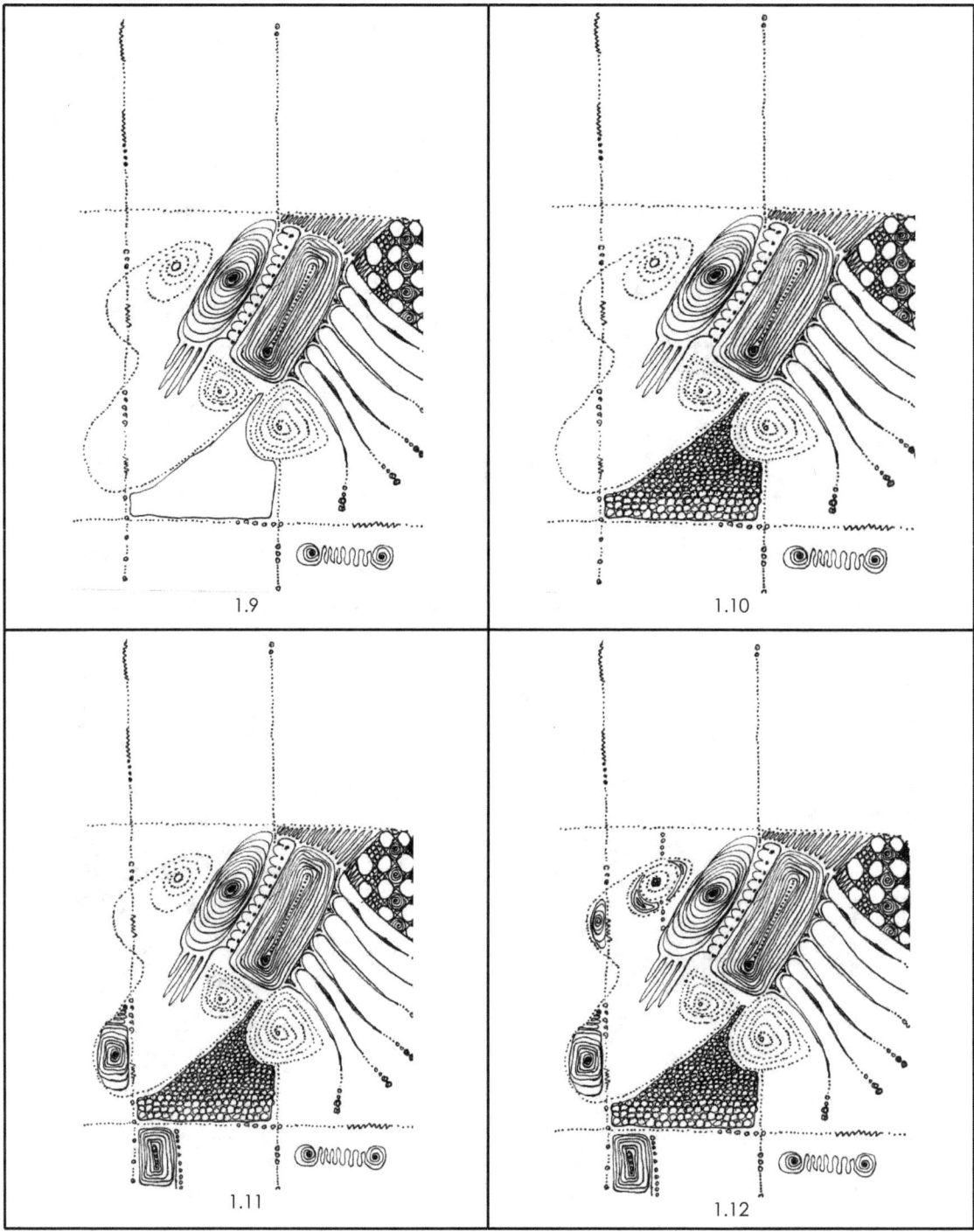

1.9

1.10

1.11

1.12

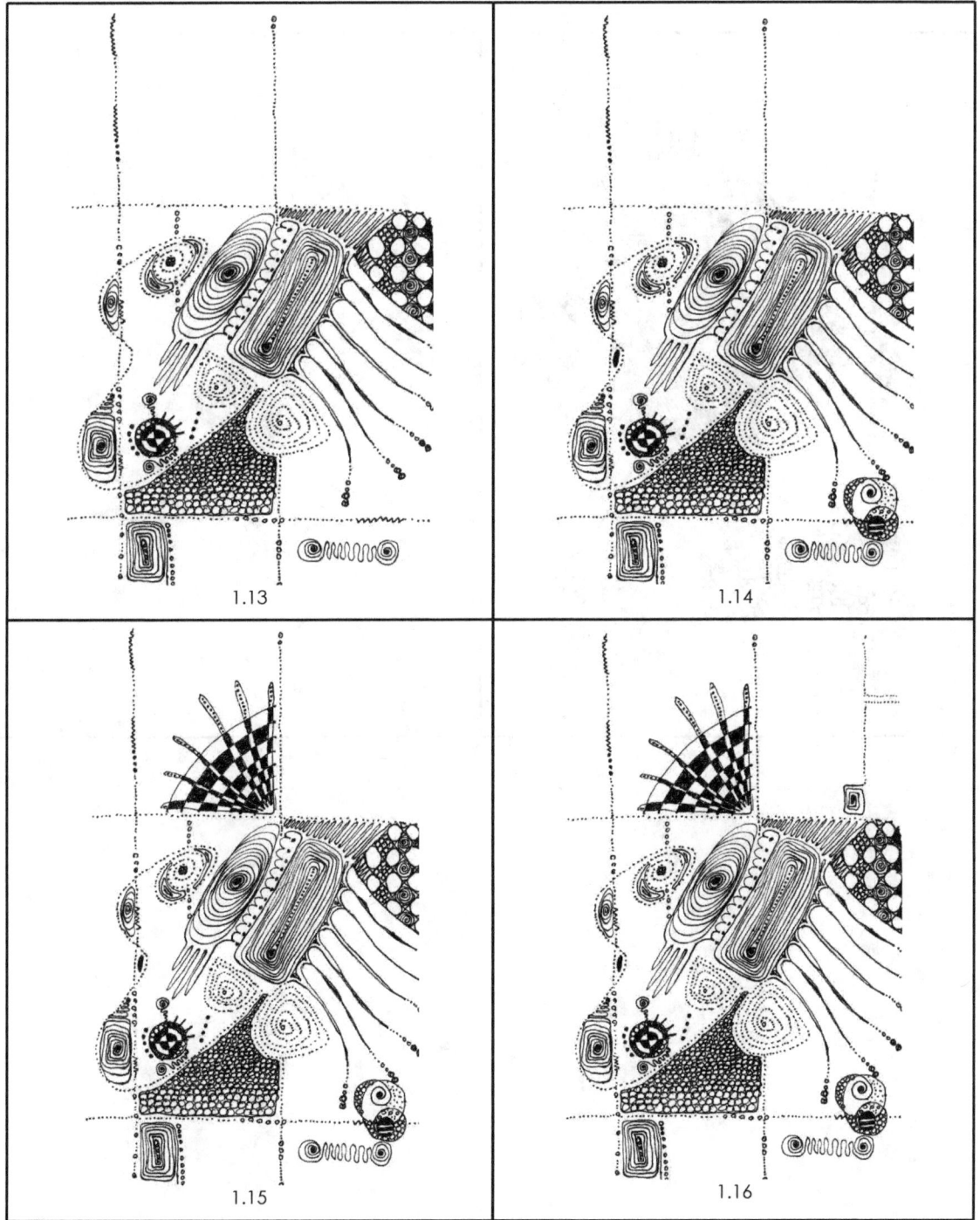

1.13

1.14

1.15

1.16

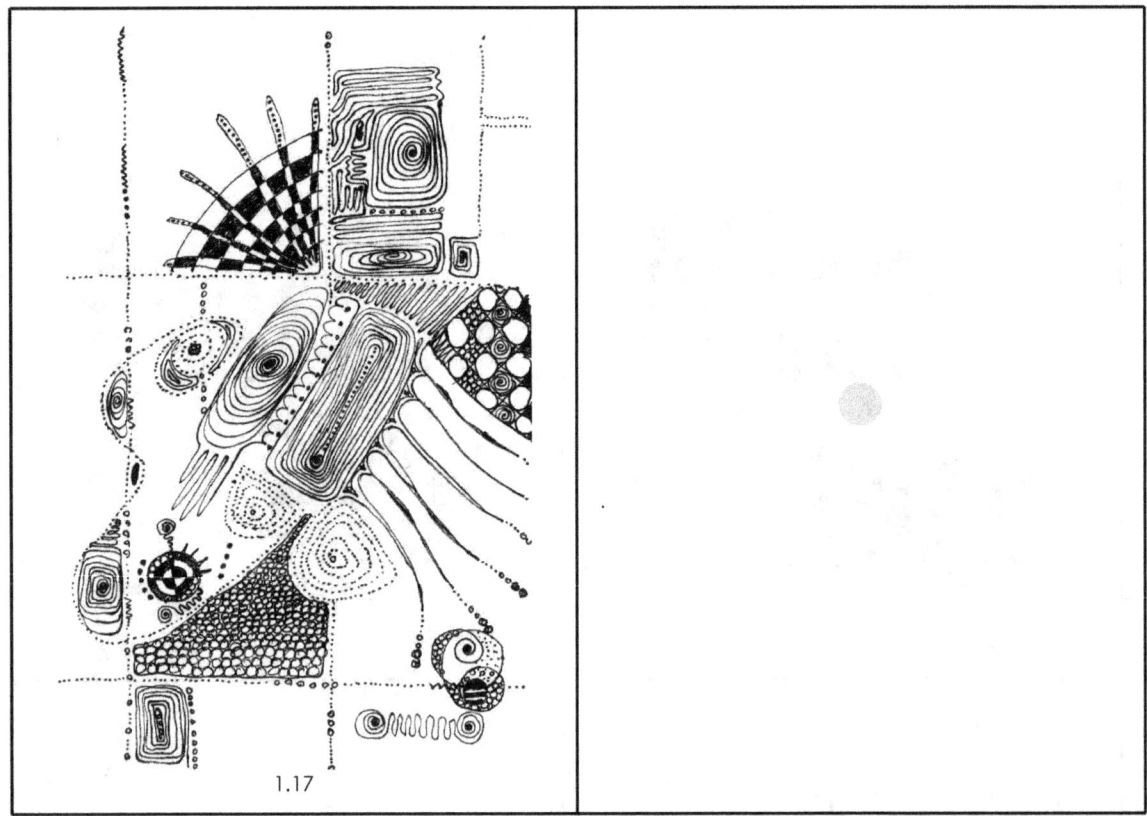

1.17

The following pages (19-23) will show you how to draw repetitive patterns, used in NeoPopRealist ink *Abstract C*. Each following image of each pattern includes new detail(s). The complicated looking drawing made with seemed simple patterns.

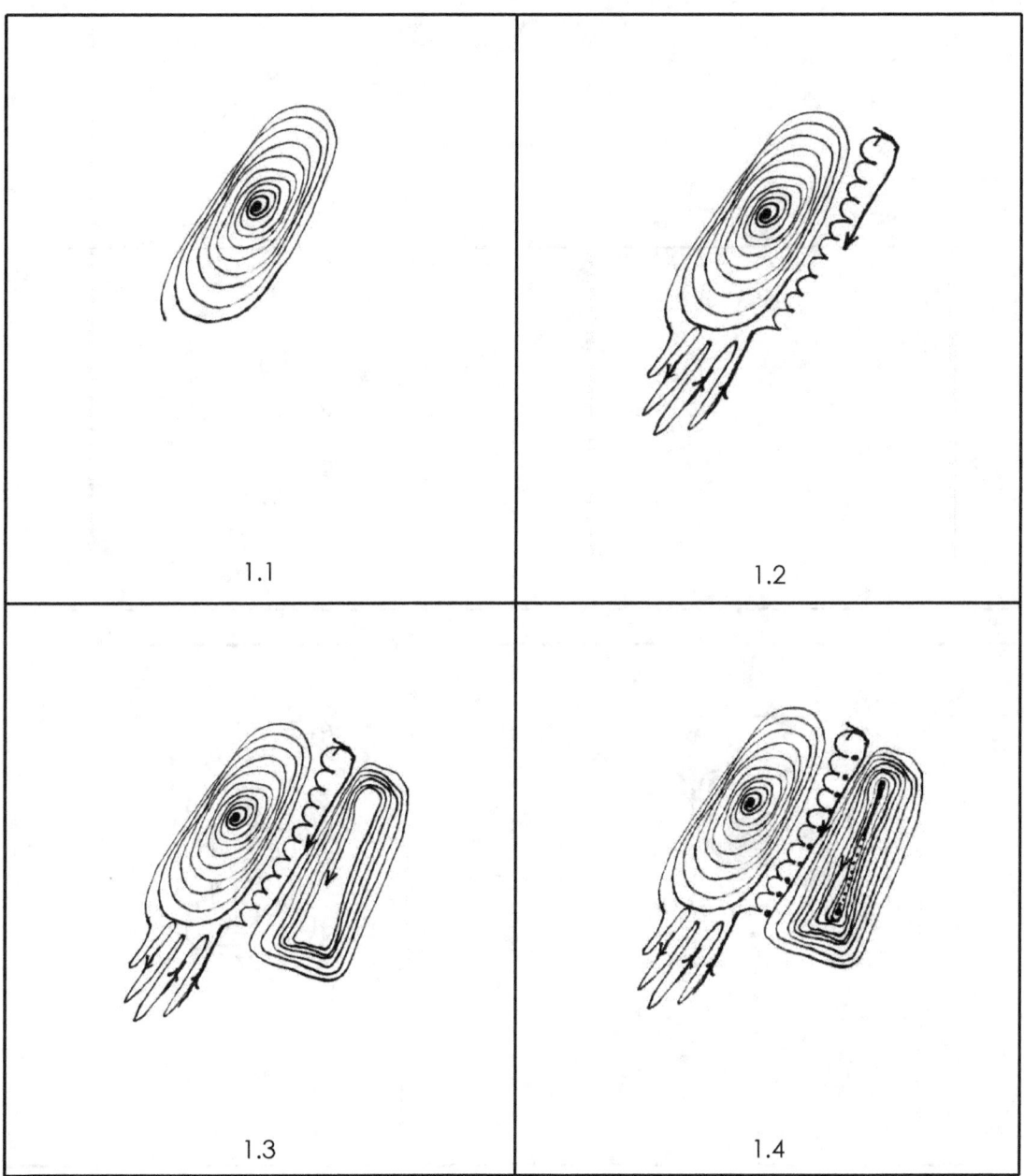

1.1

1.2

1.3

1.4

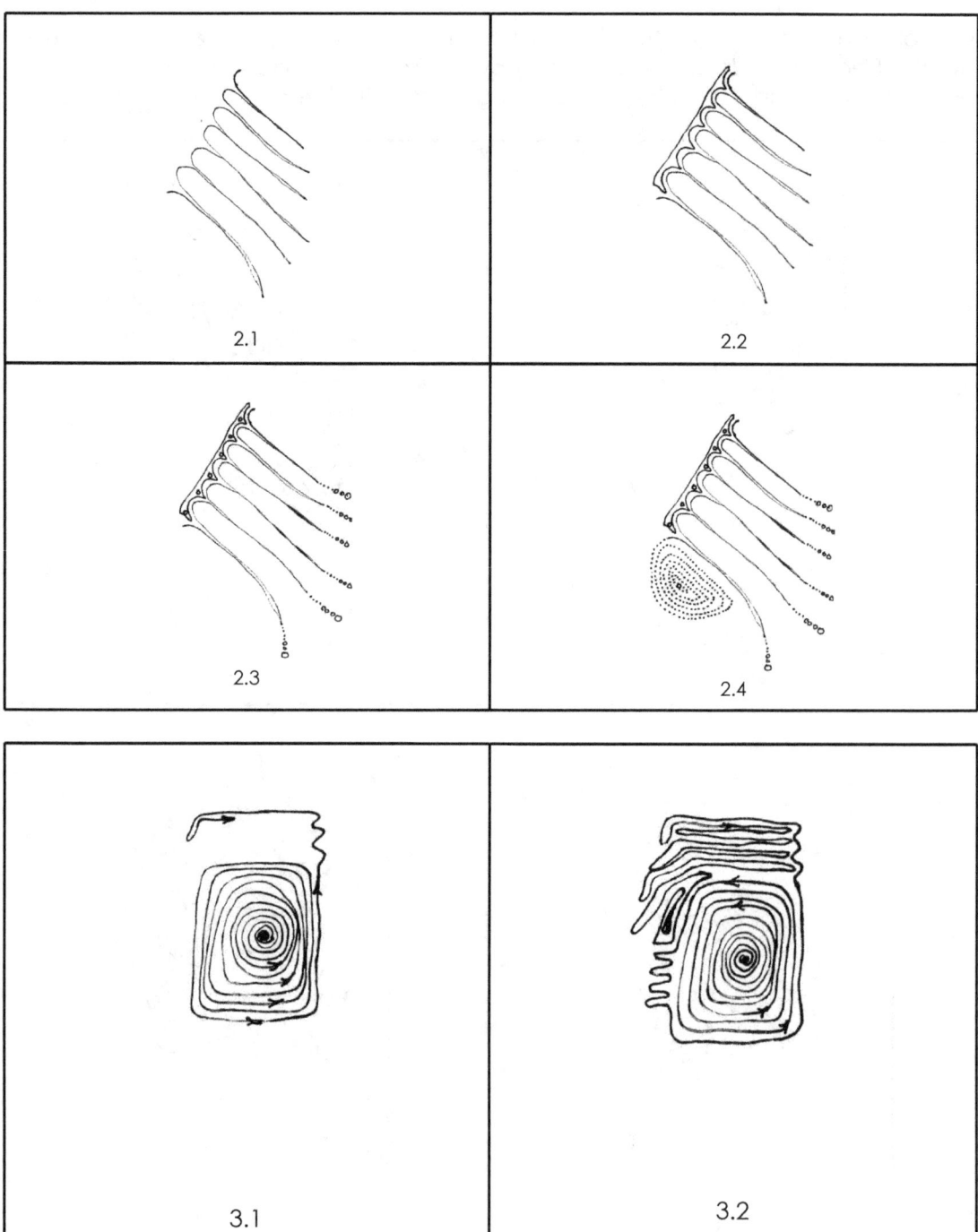

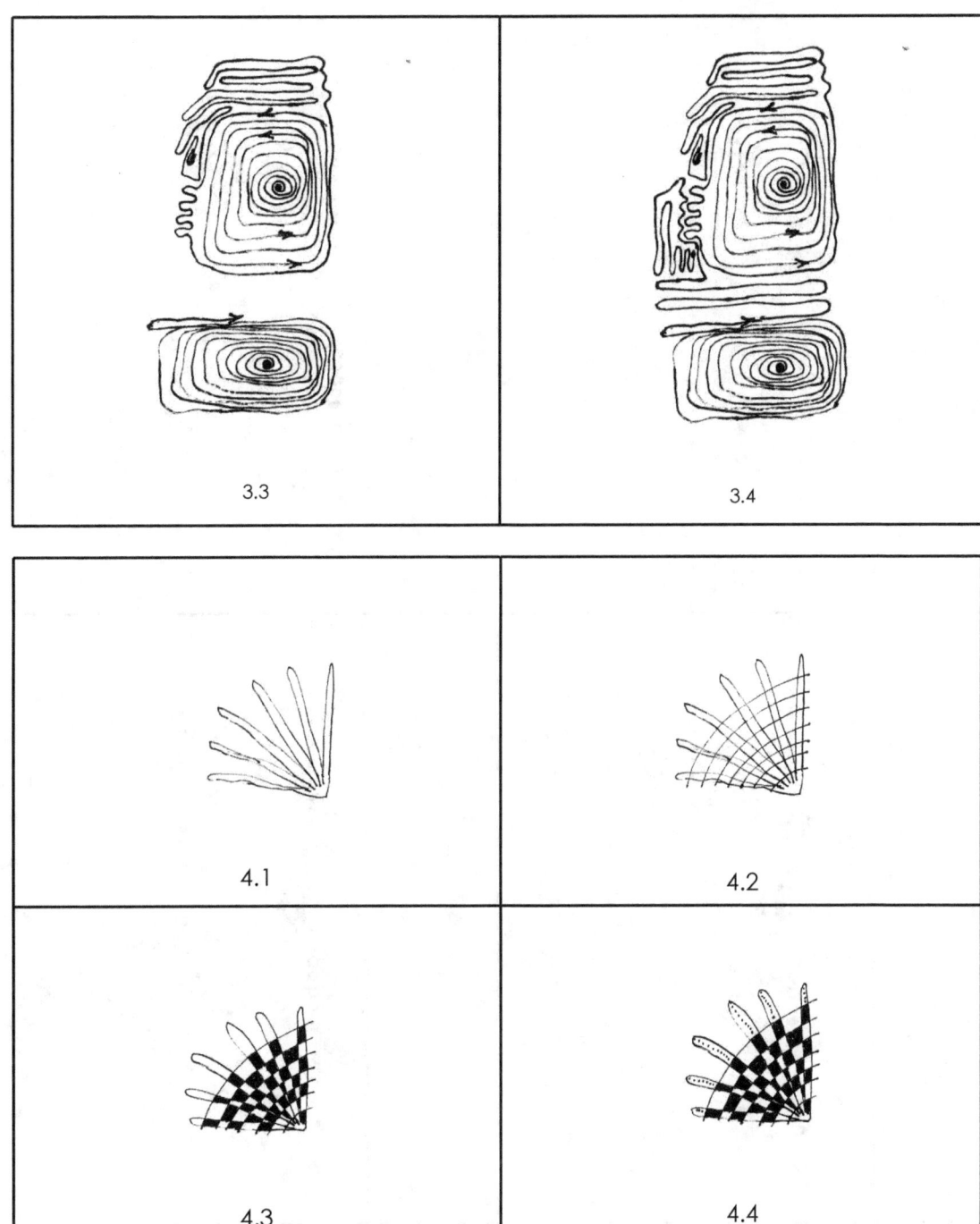

3.3

3.4

4.1

4.2

4,3

4.4

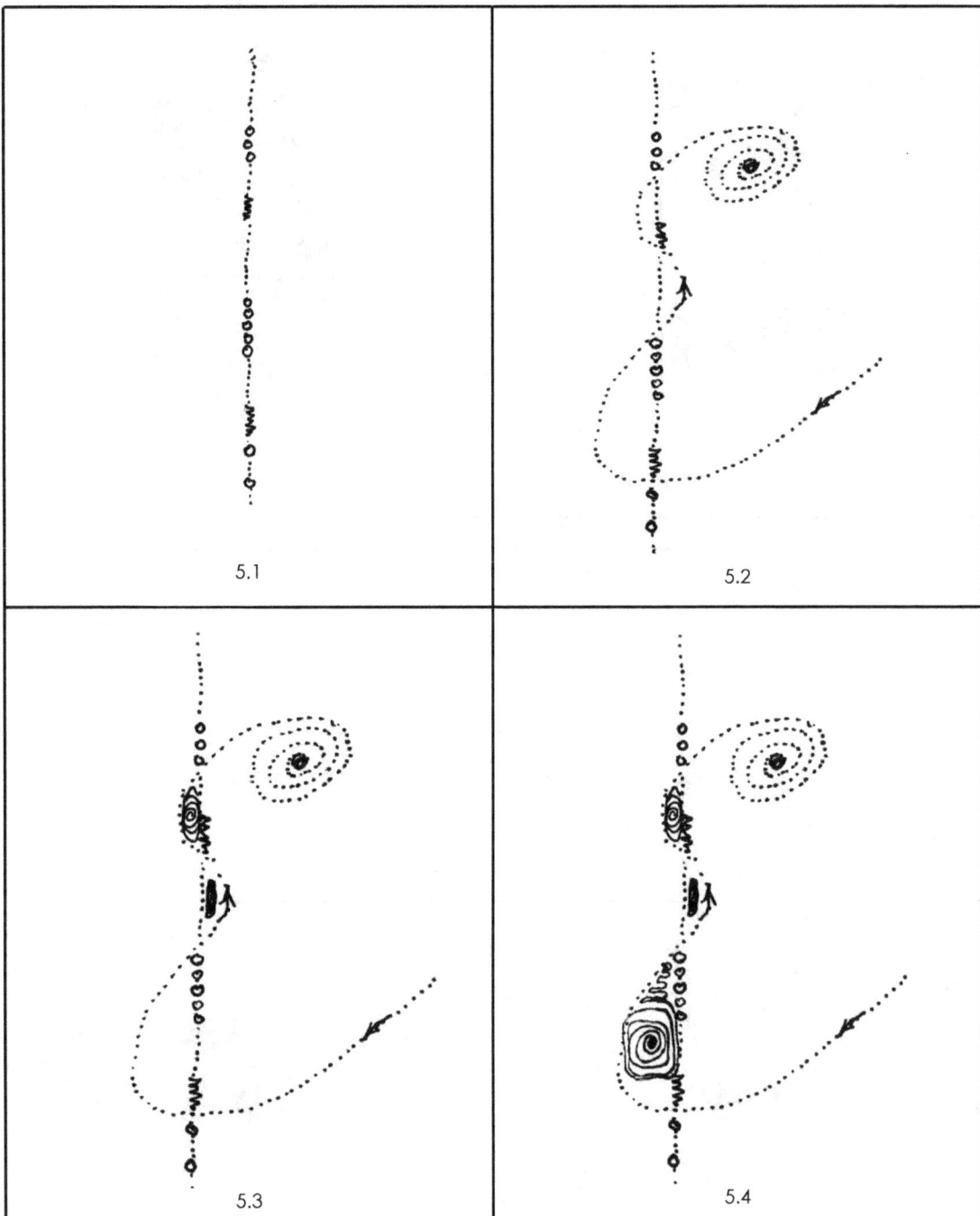

5.1

5.2

5.3

5.4

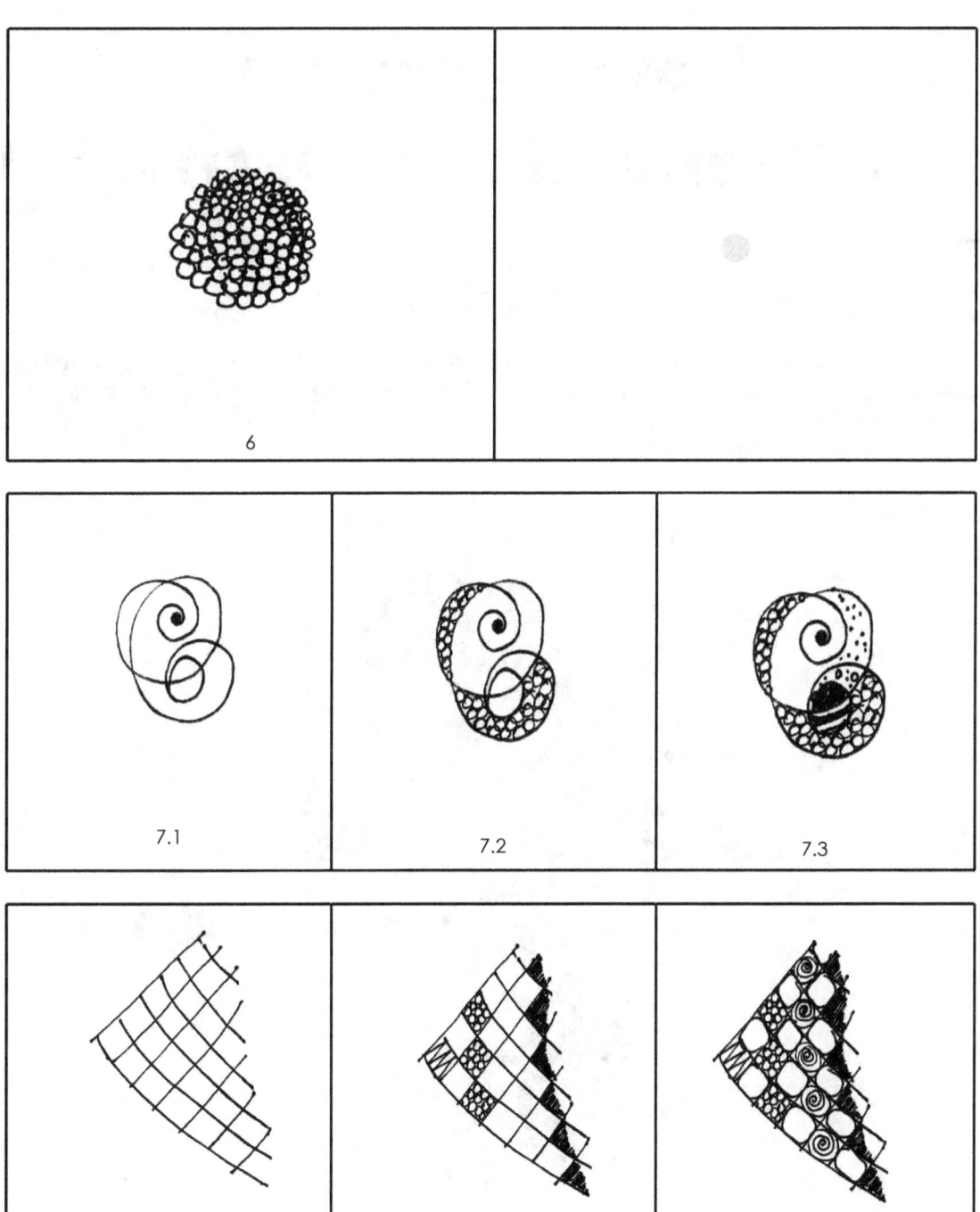

6

7.1

7.2

7.3

8.1

8.2

8.3

How to create NeoPopRealism Abstract D

The following pages will show step-by-step how to create NeoPopRealism advanced *Abstract D* which can be used as the background in a drawing. Also, such abstract can be presented as the independent ink design. To create such abstracts you need imagination and artistic skills. Every following picture includes new additional detail(s); the final abstract looks like this:

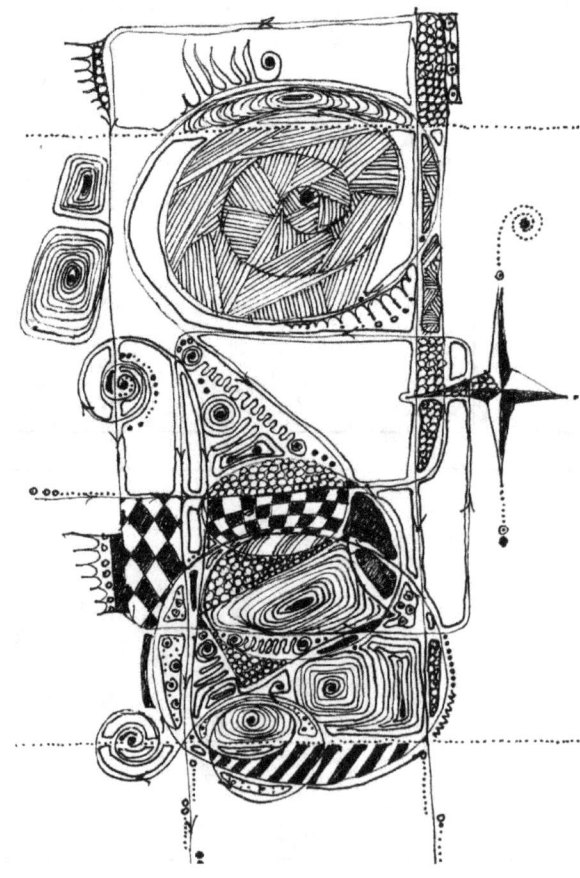

Abstract D, ink on paper

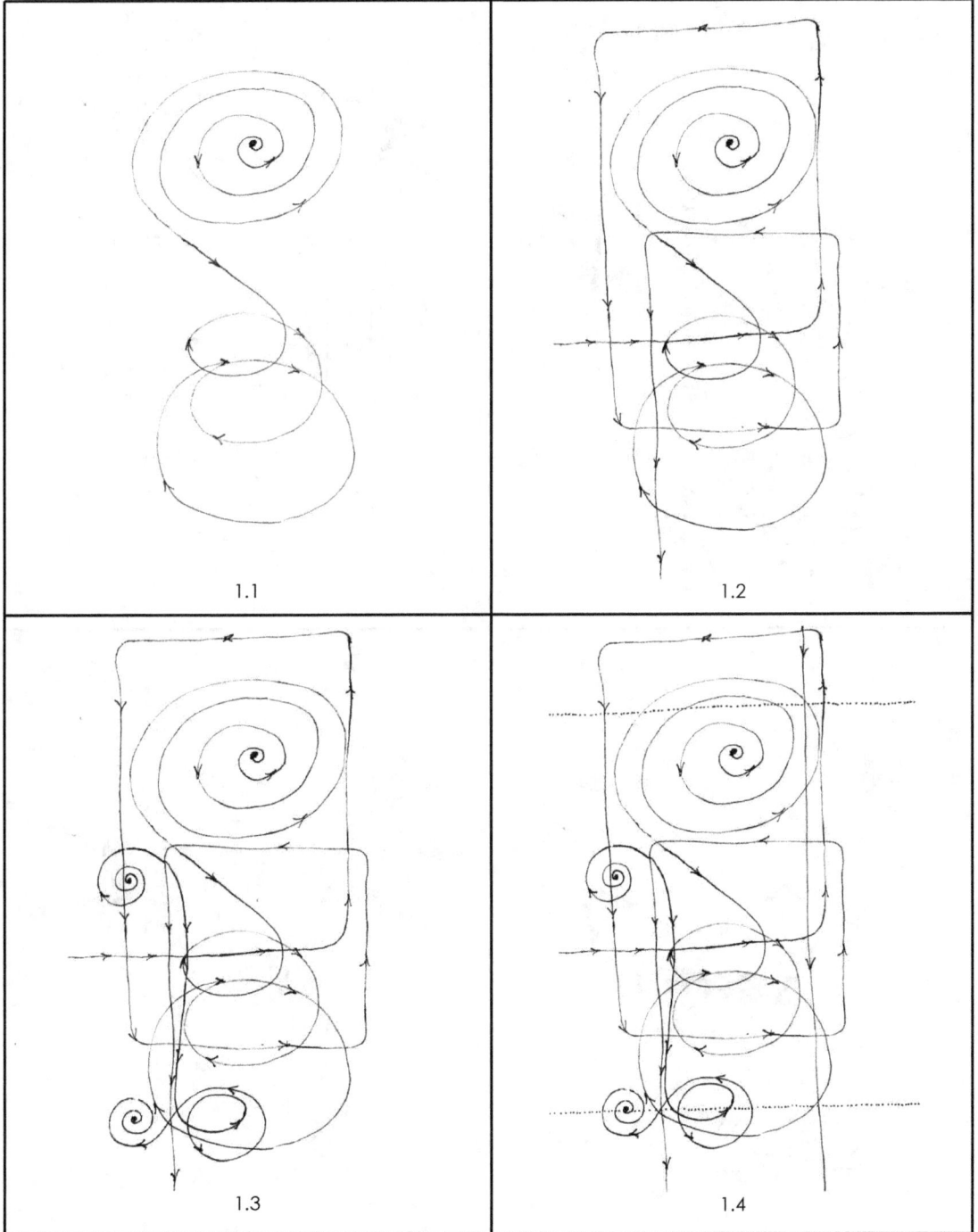

1.1

1.2

1.3

1.4

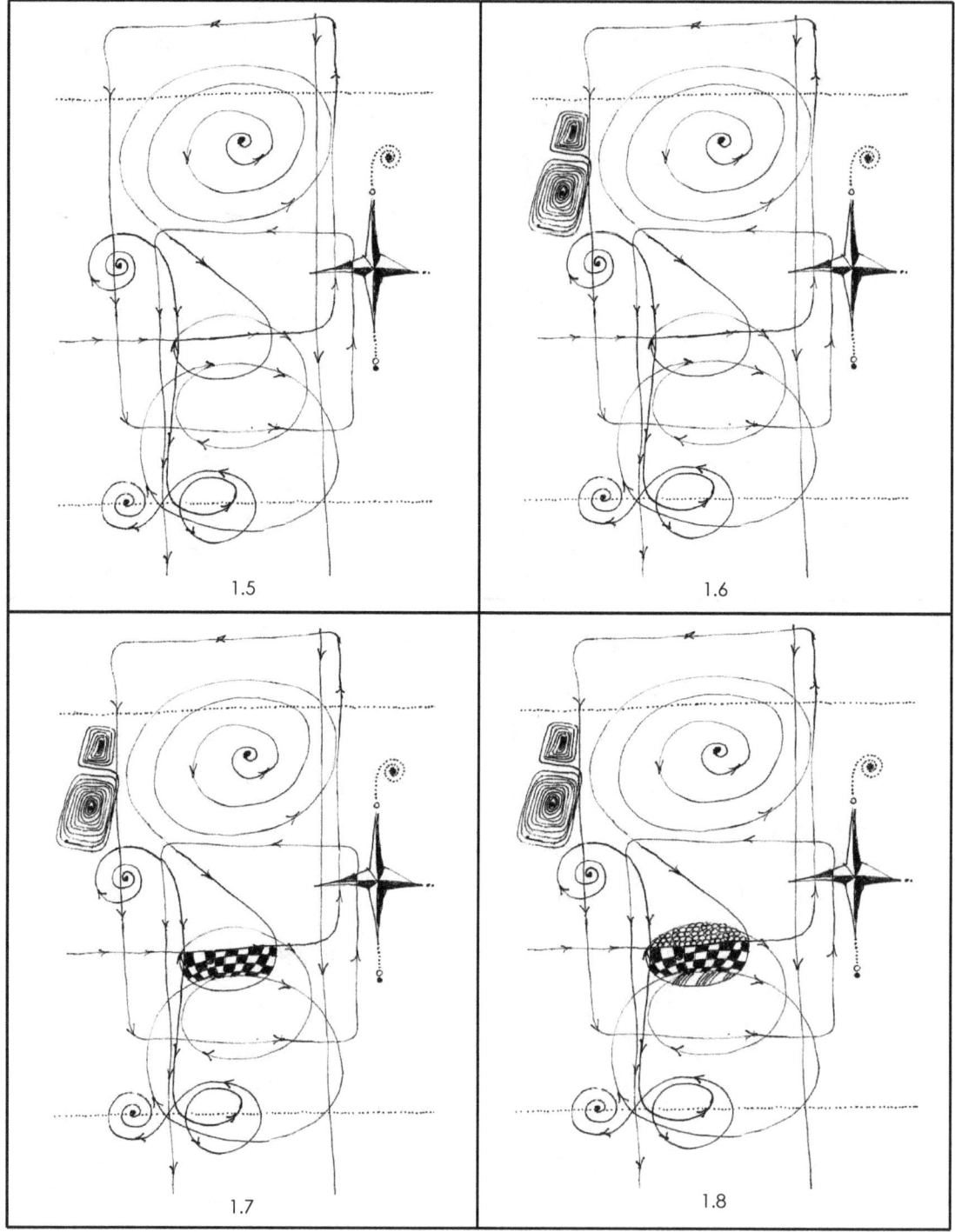

1.5

1.6

1.7

1.8

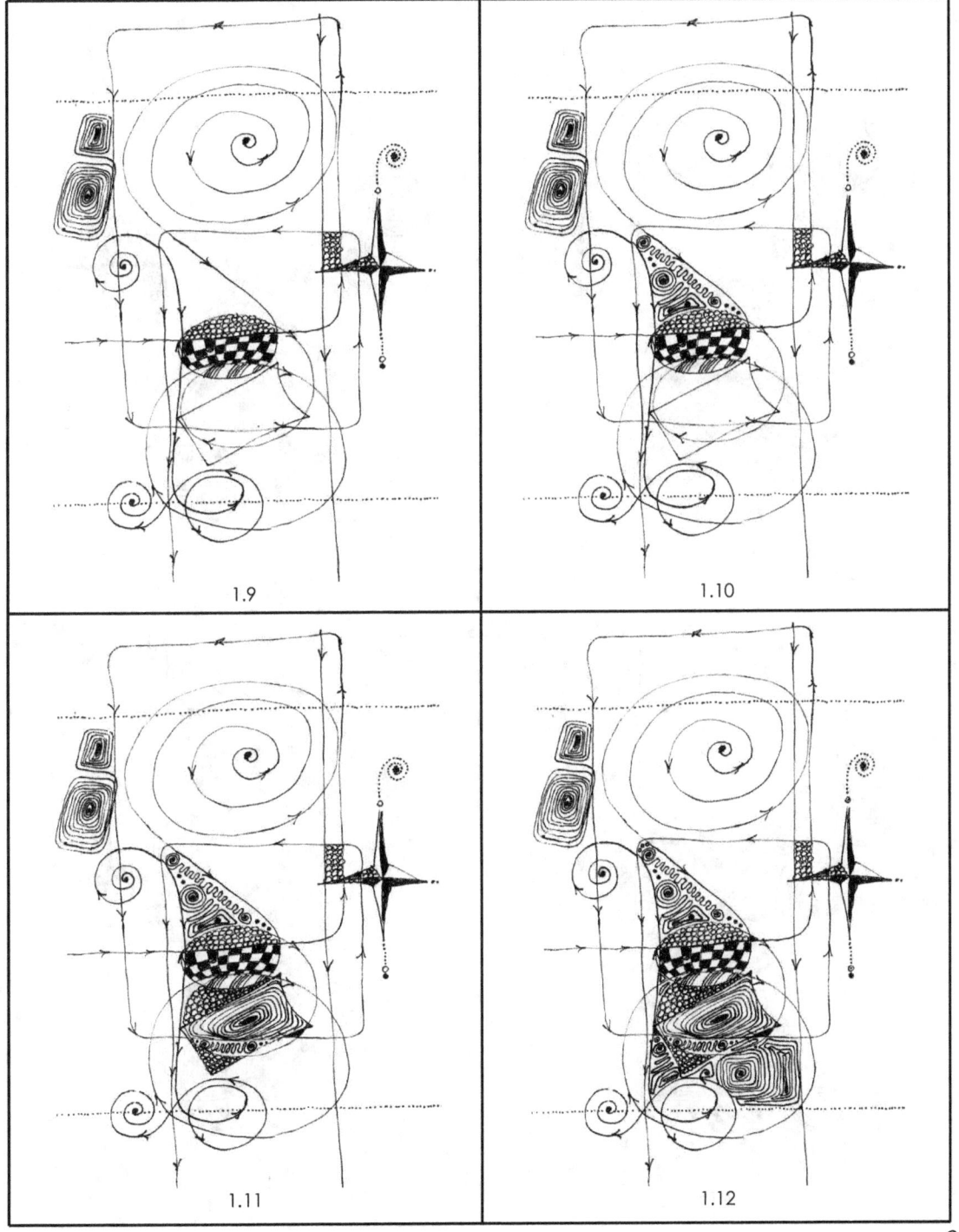

1.9

1.10

1.11

1.12

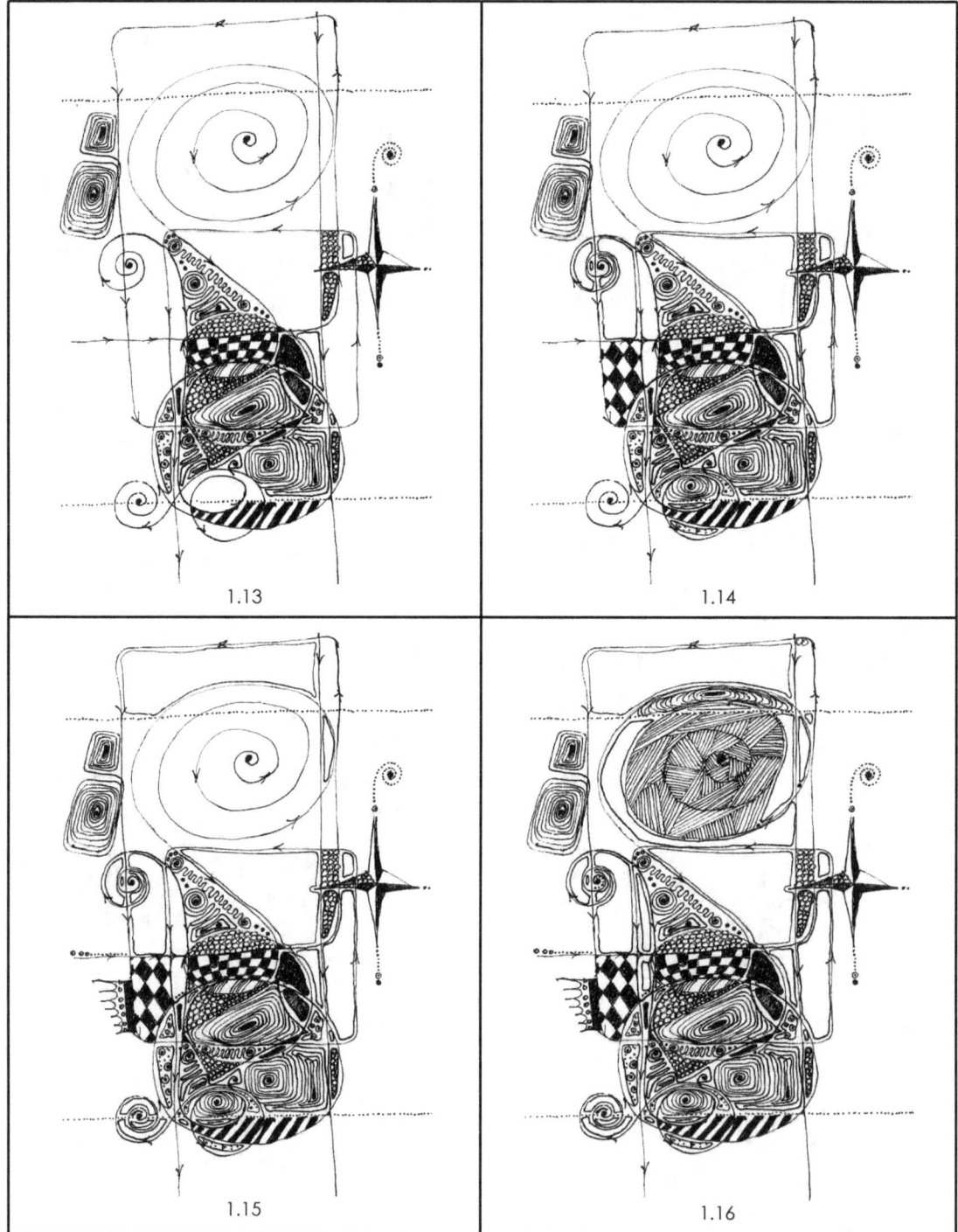

1.13

1.14

1.15

1.16

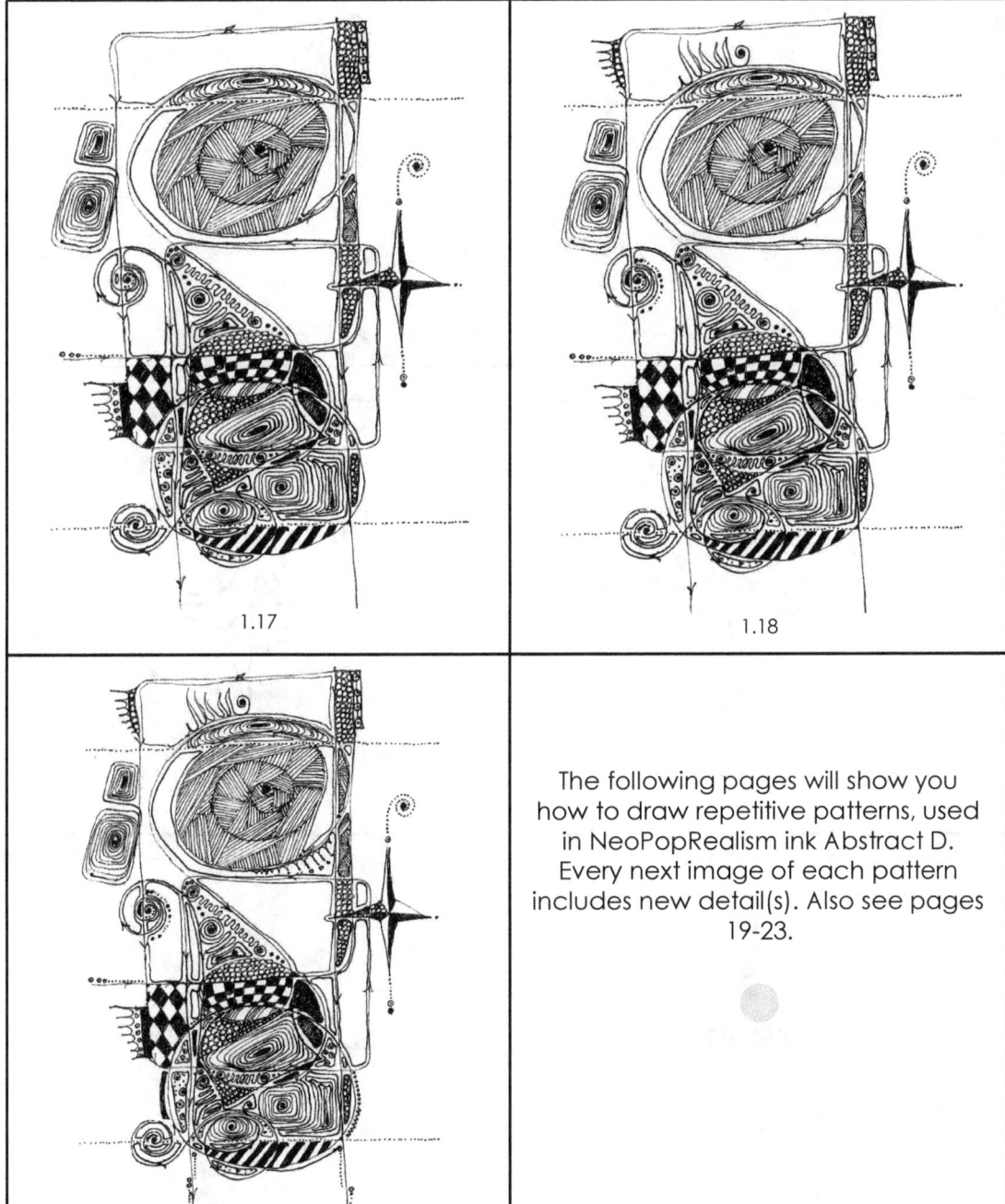

1.17

1.18

1.19

The following pages will show you how to draw repetitive patterns, used in NeoPopRealism ink Abstract D. Every next image of each pattern includes new detail(s). Also see pages 19-23.

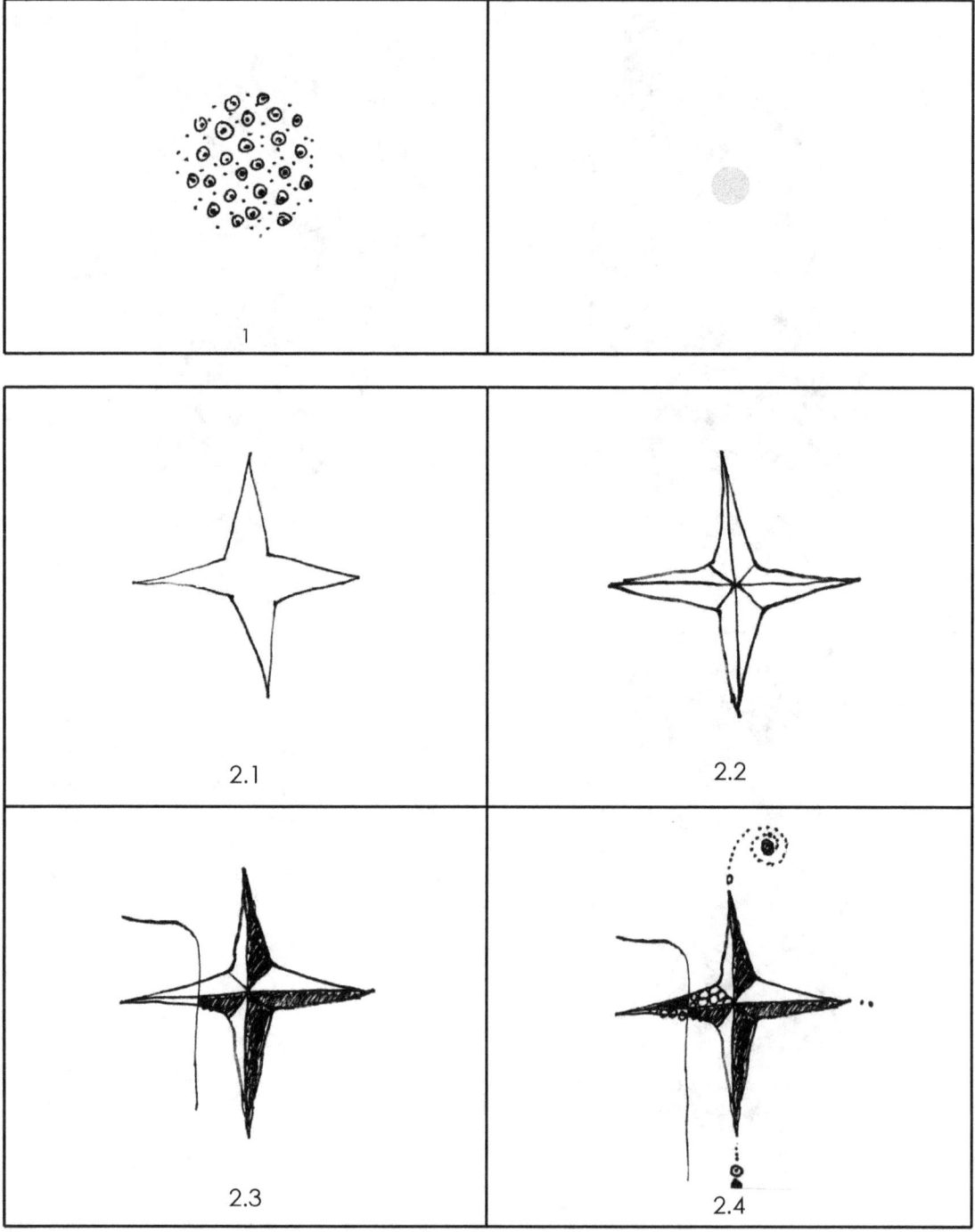

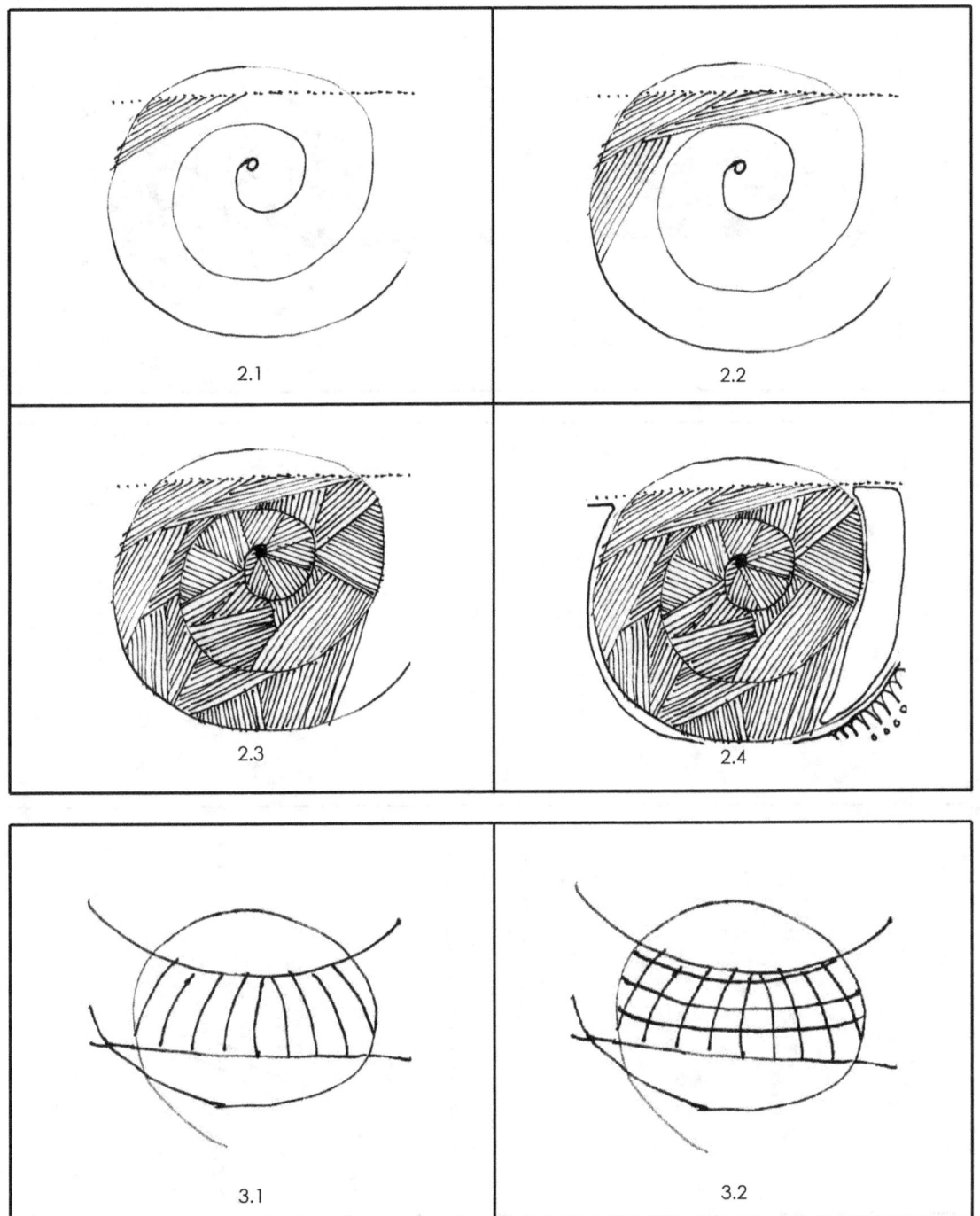

2.1

2.2

2.3

2.4

3.1

3.2

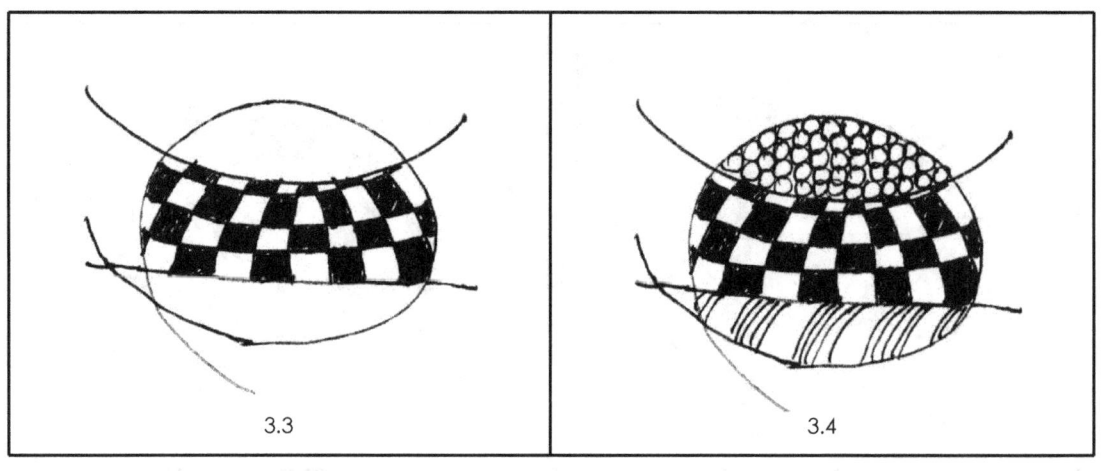

3.3

3.4

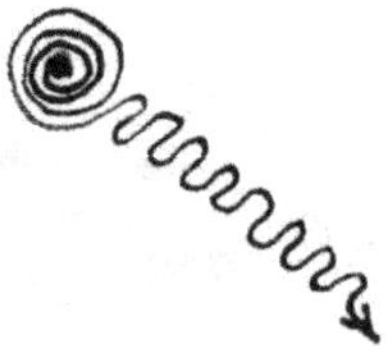

4.1

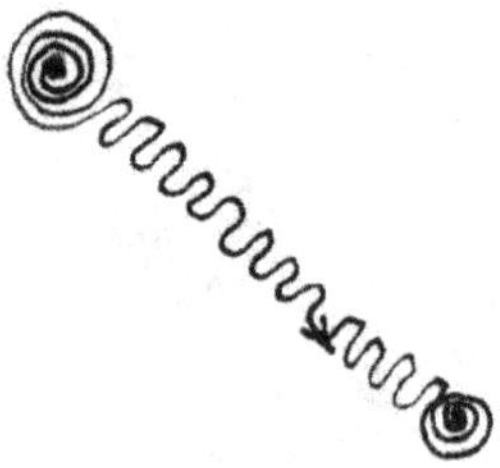

4.2

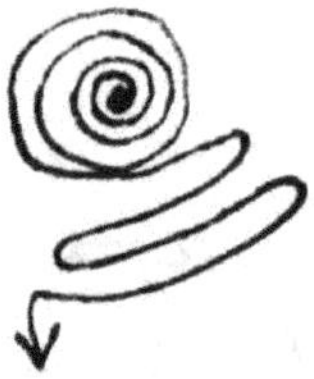

5.1

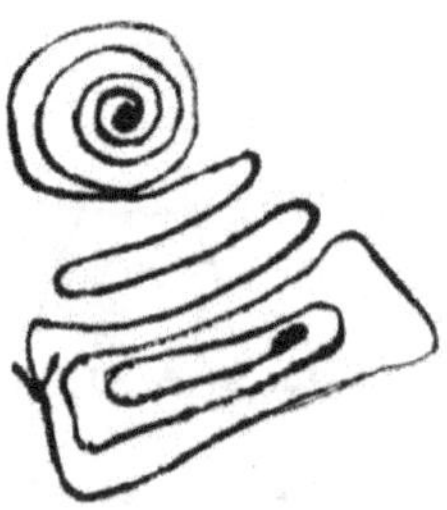

5.2

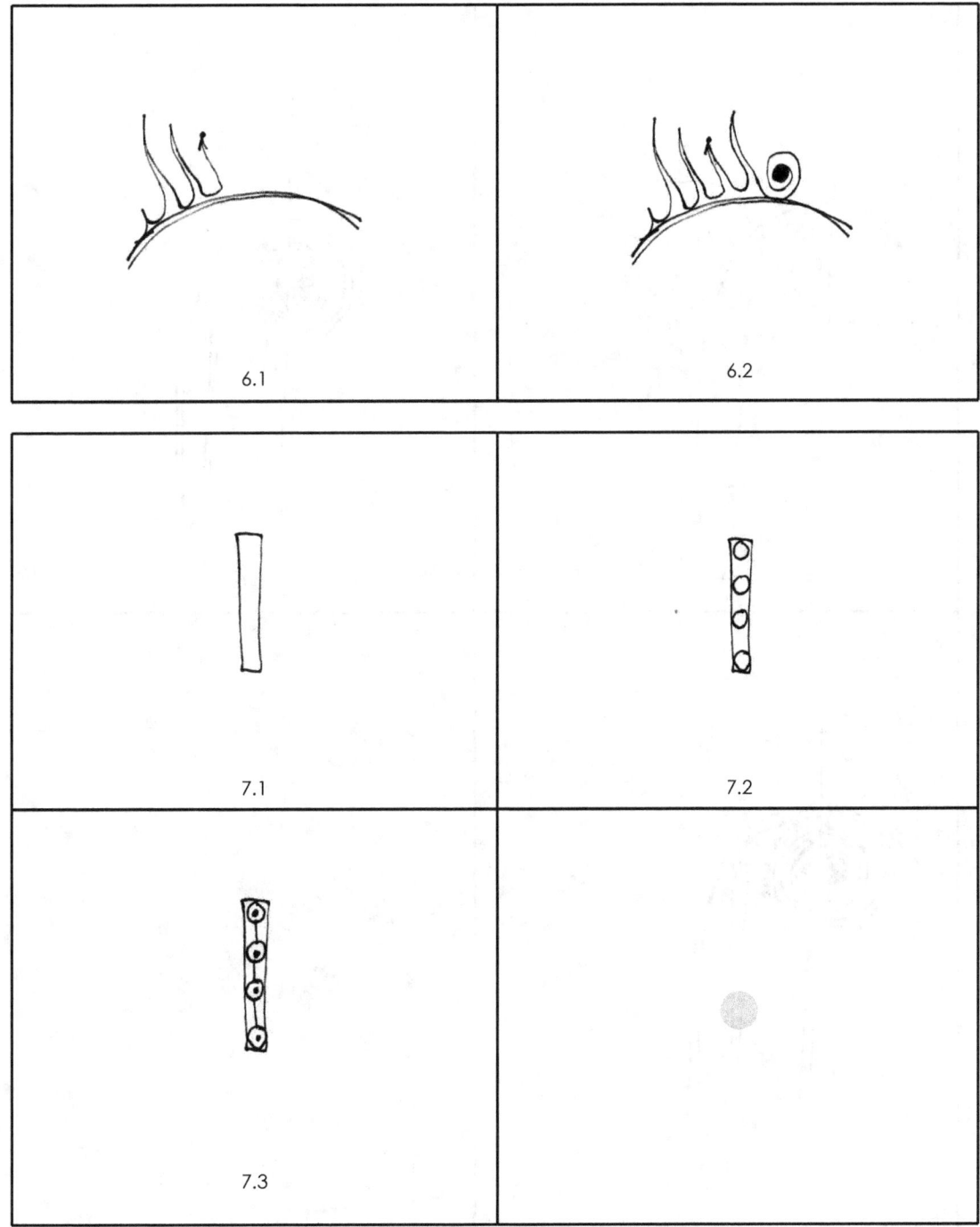

6.1

6.2

7.1

7.2

7.3

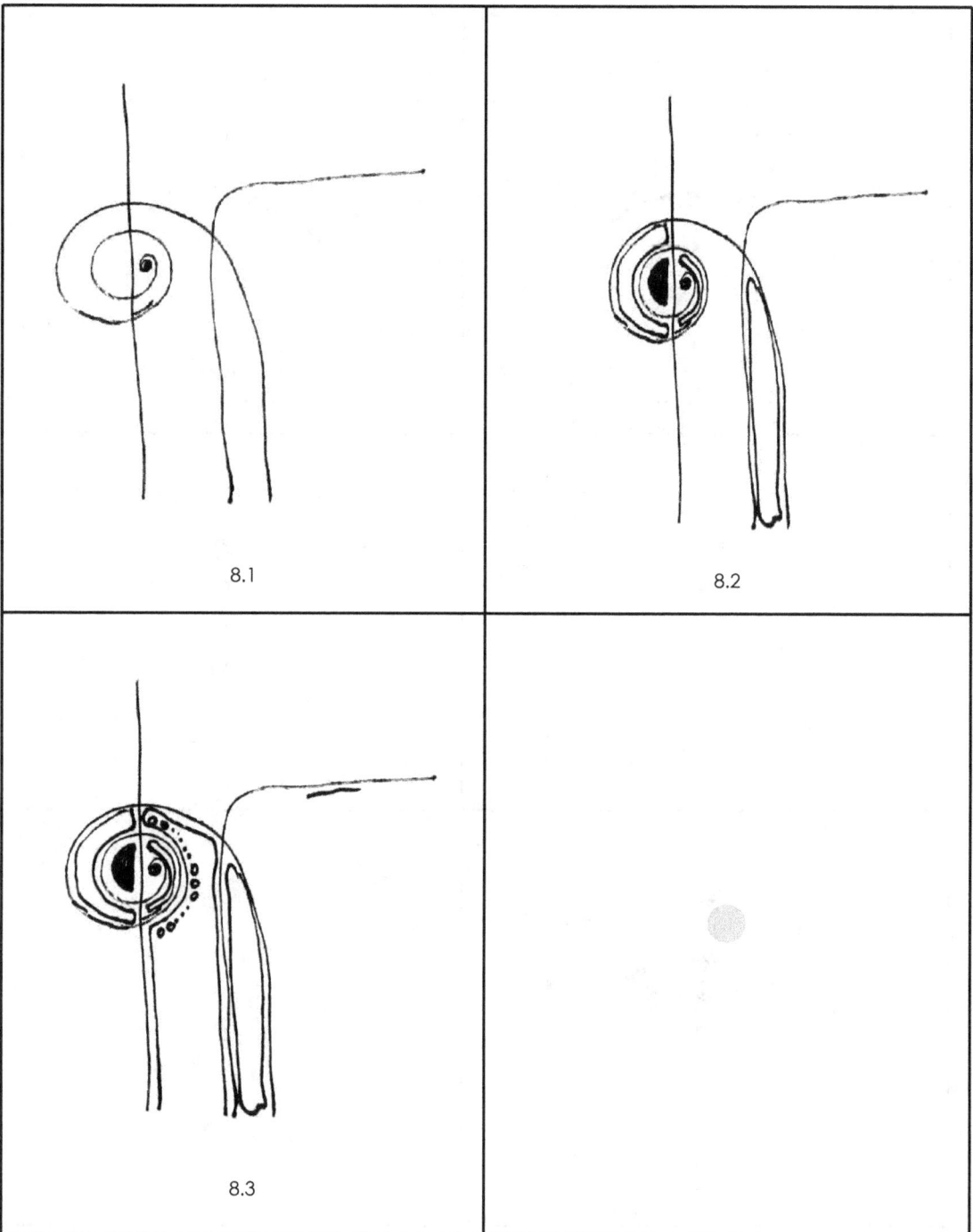

8.1

8.2

8.3

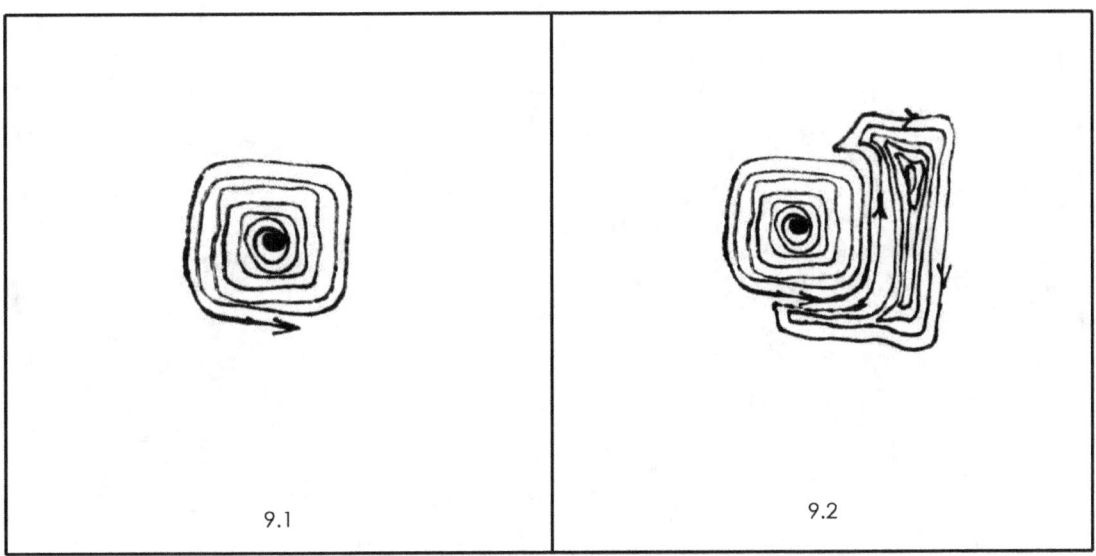

9.1   9.2

HOW TO DRAW NEOPOPREALISM ADVANCED ABSTRACT IMAGES

Create abstracts with Nadia Russ

The following pages (39-60) invite you to draw abstracts with Nadia Russ here and now. All you need is the thin ink pen because thick pen will leave marks on another side of the page. Complete sections of the following abstracts with the offered repetitive patterns or use your imagination and create new ones.

When you draw repetitive patterns, you enter the meditative state of mind. Meditation is a positive brain-changing activity that increases your brain functions. It helps people suffering from anxiety, depression, post-traumatic stress disorder, more. There's strong connection between meditation, healthier immune system and happiness. Through meditation you achieve sublime state of mind. Meditation process increases your creativity, learning abilities and memory. This drawing process helps you develop your artistic intuition, with this drawing you will learn how to create balanced and interesting compositions. Create, improvise, experiment!

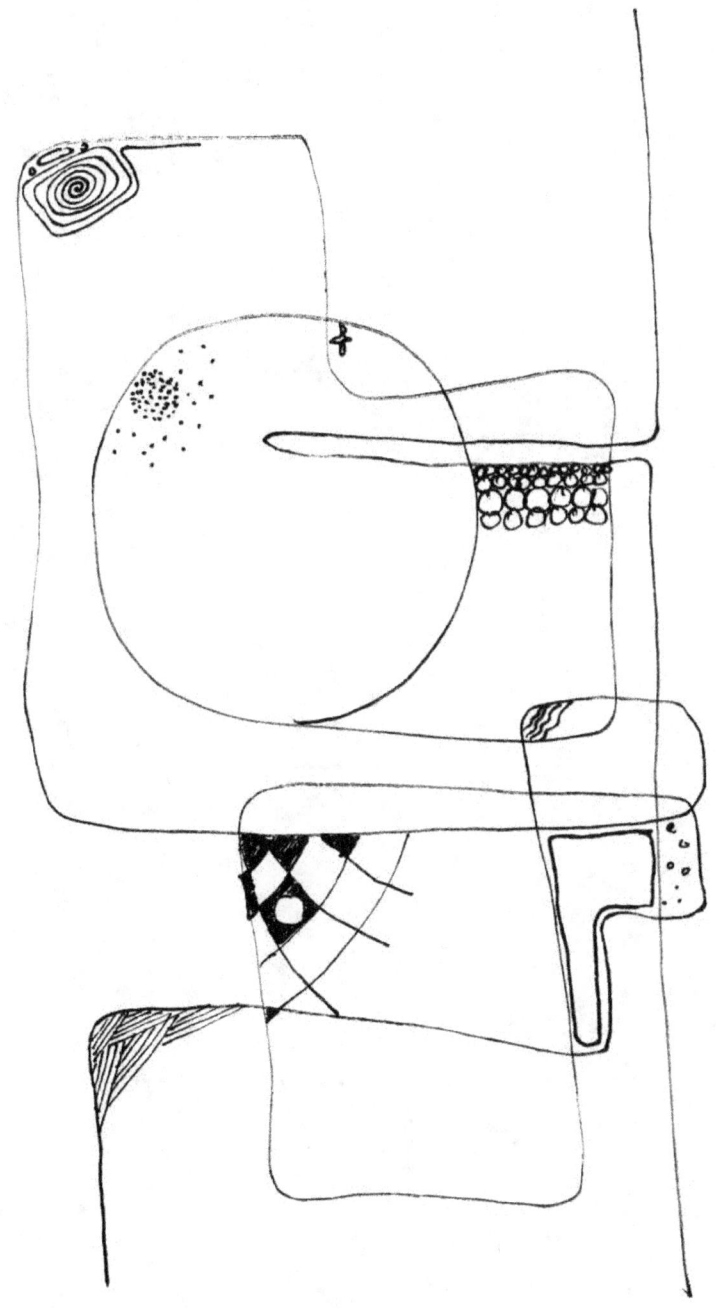

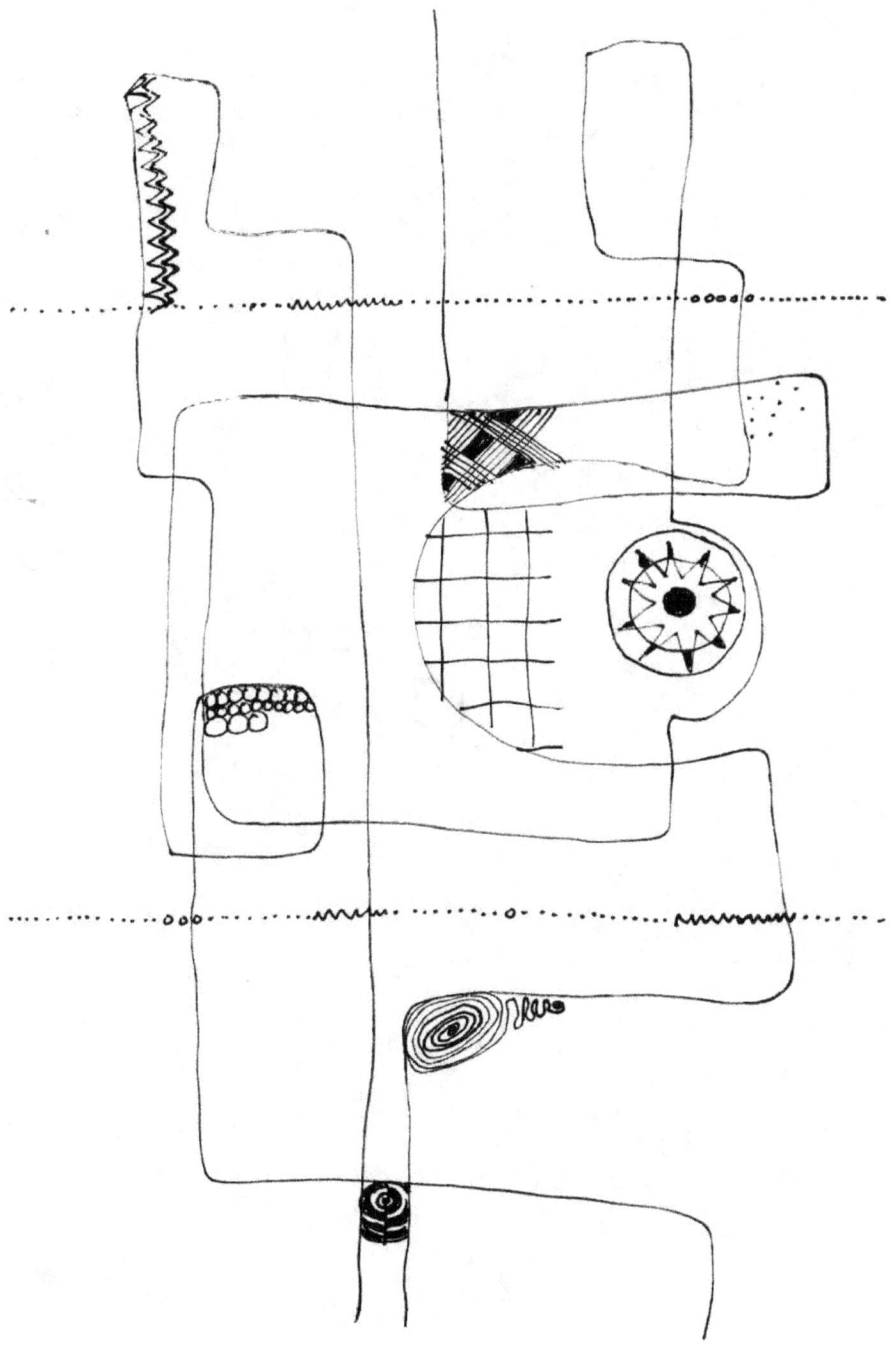

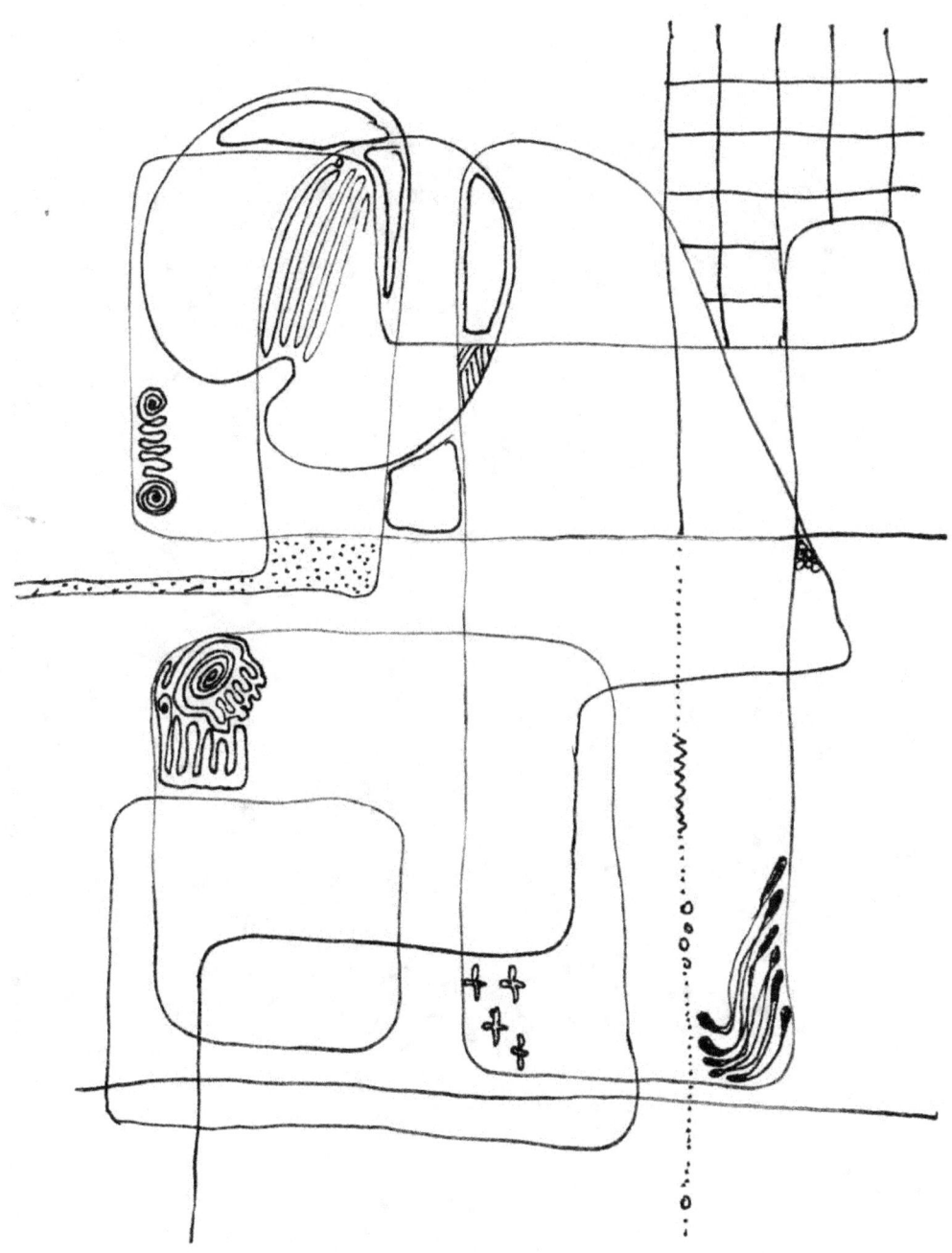

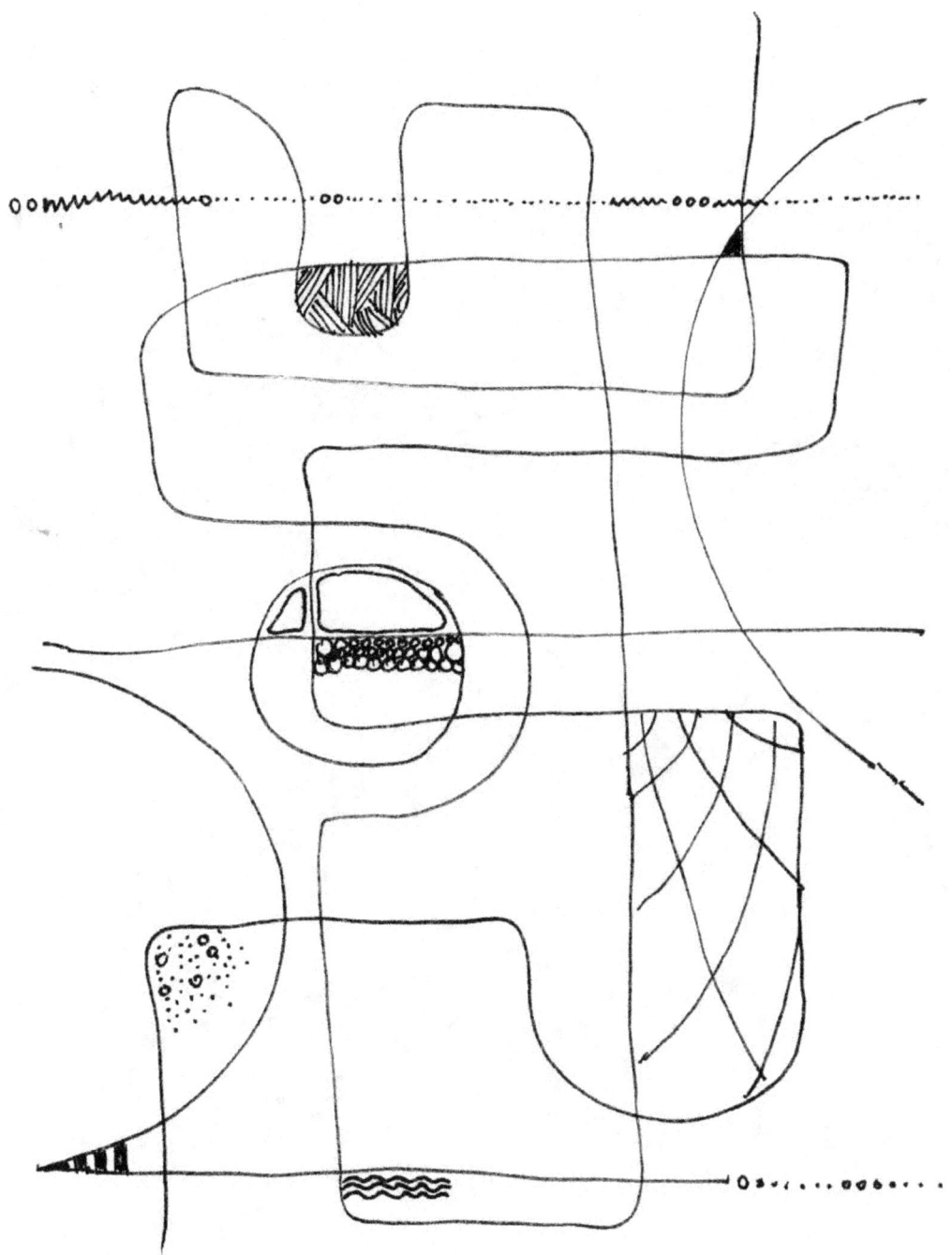

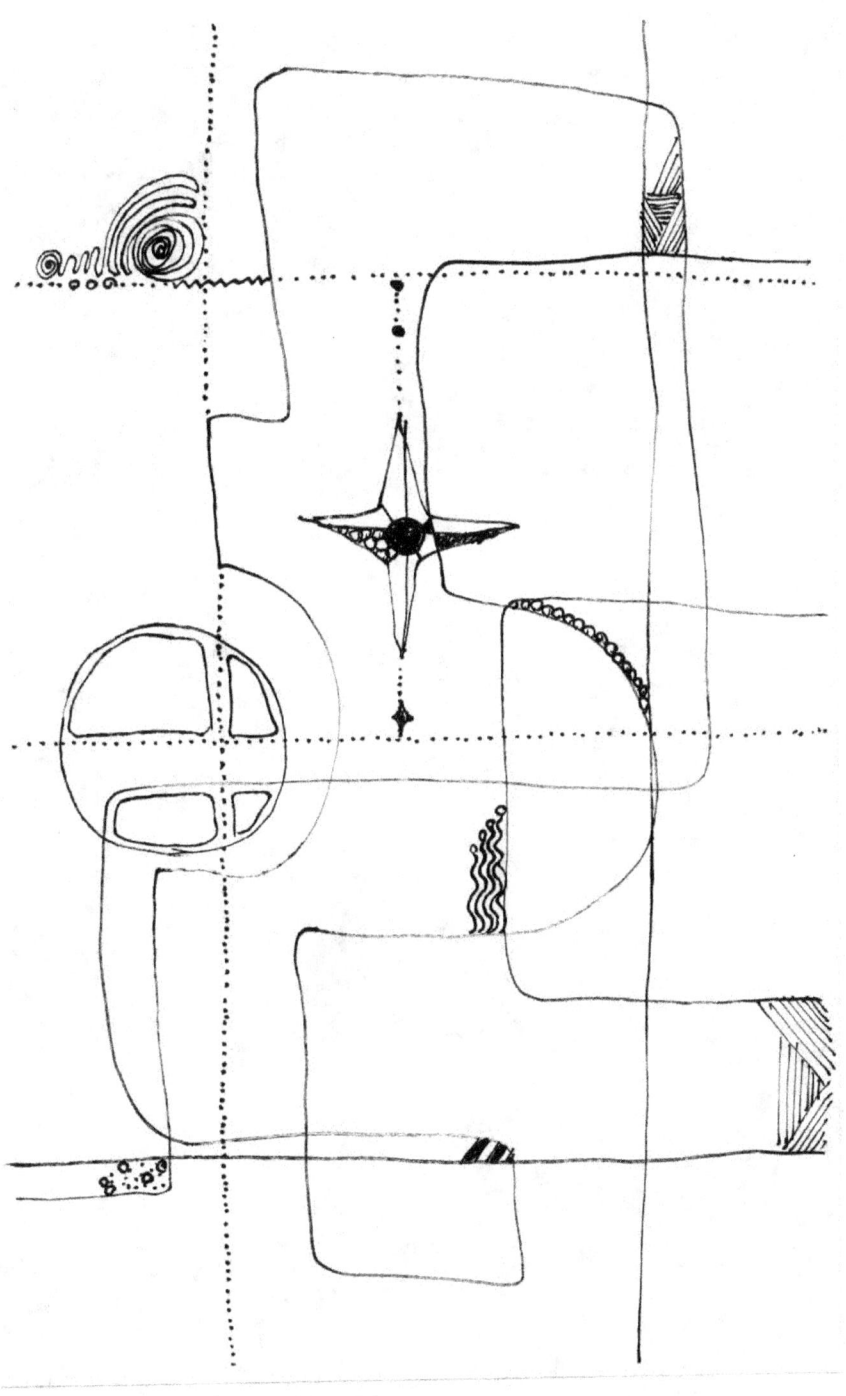

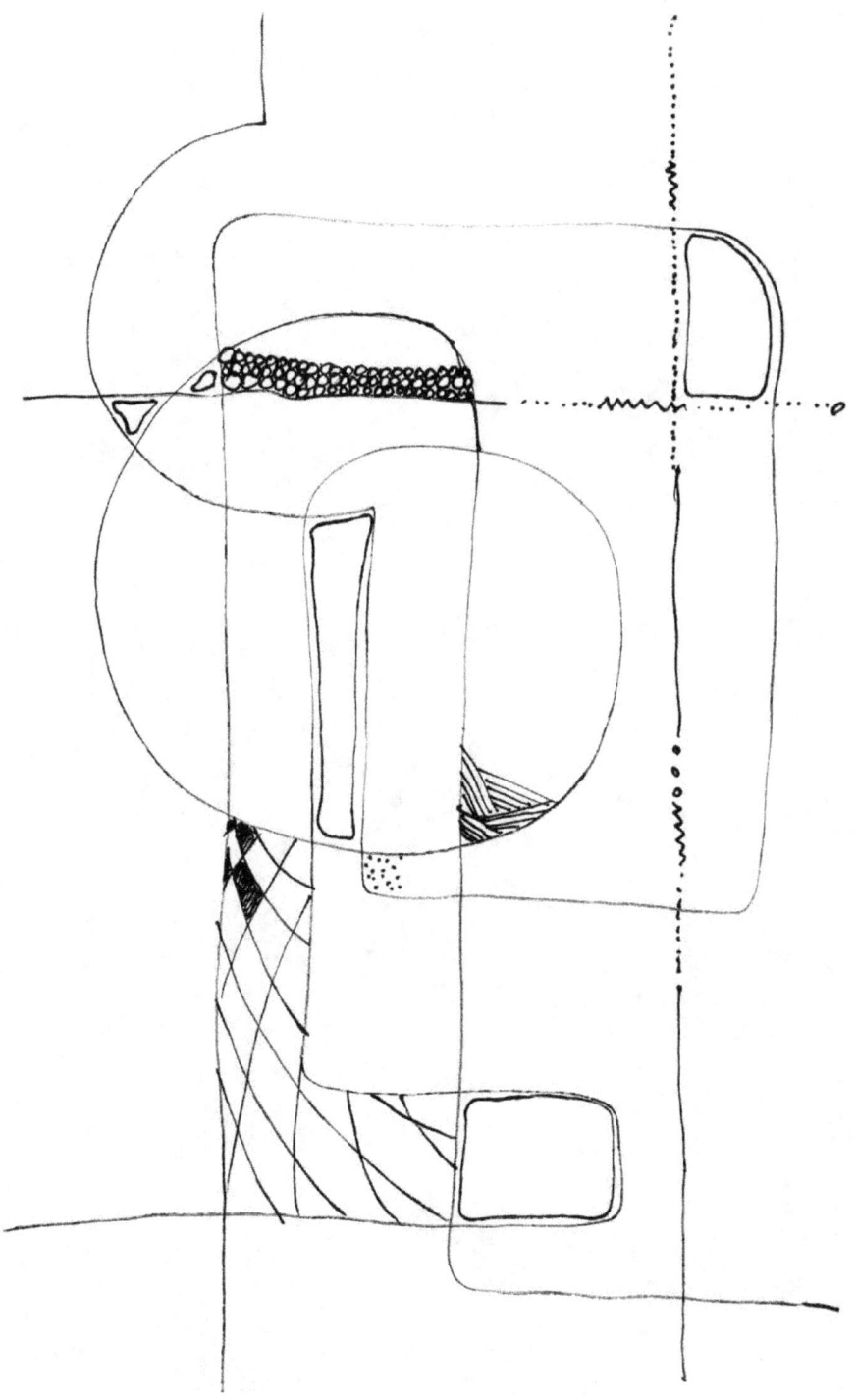

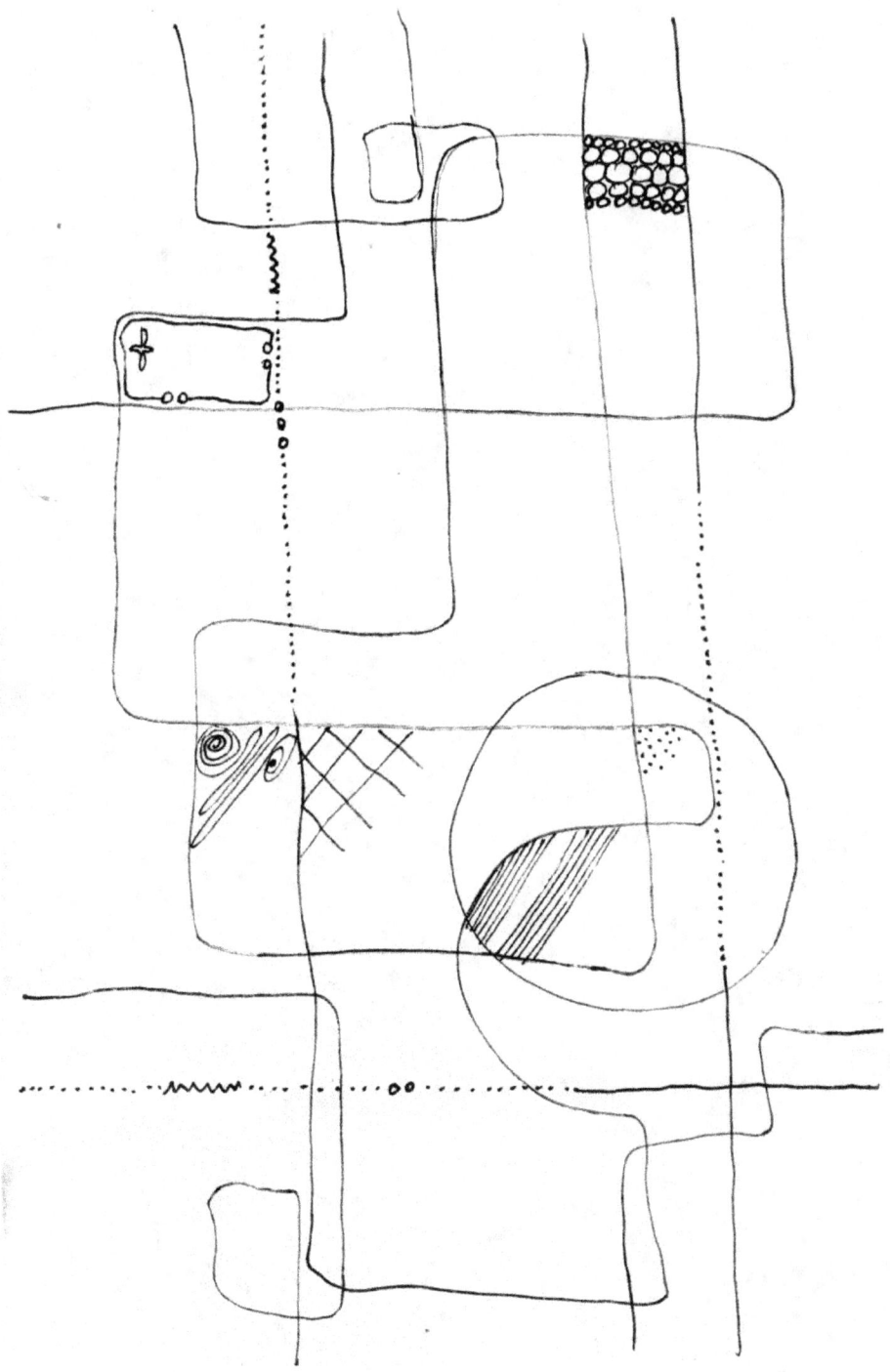

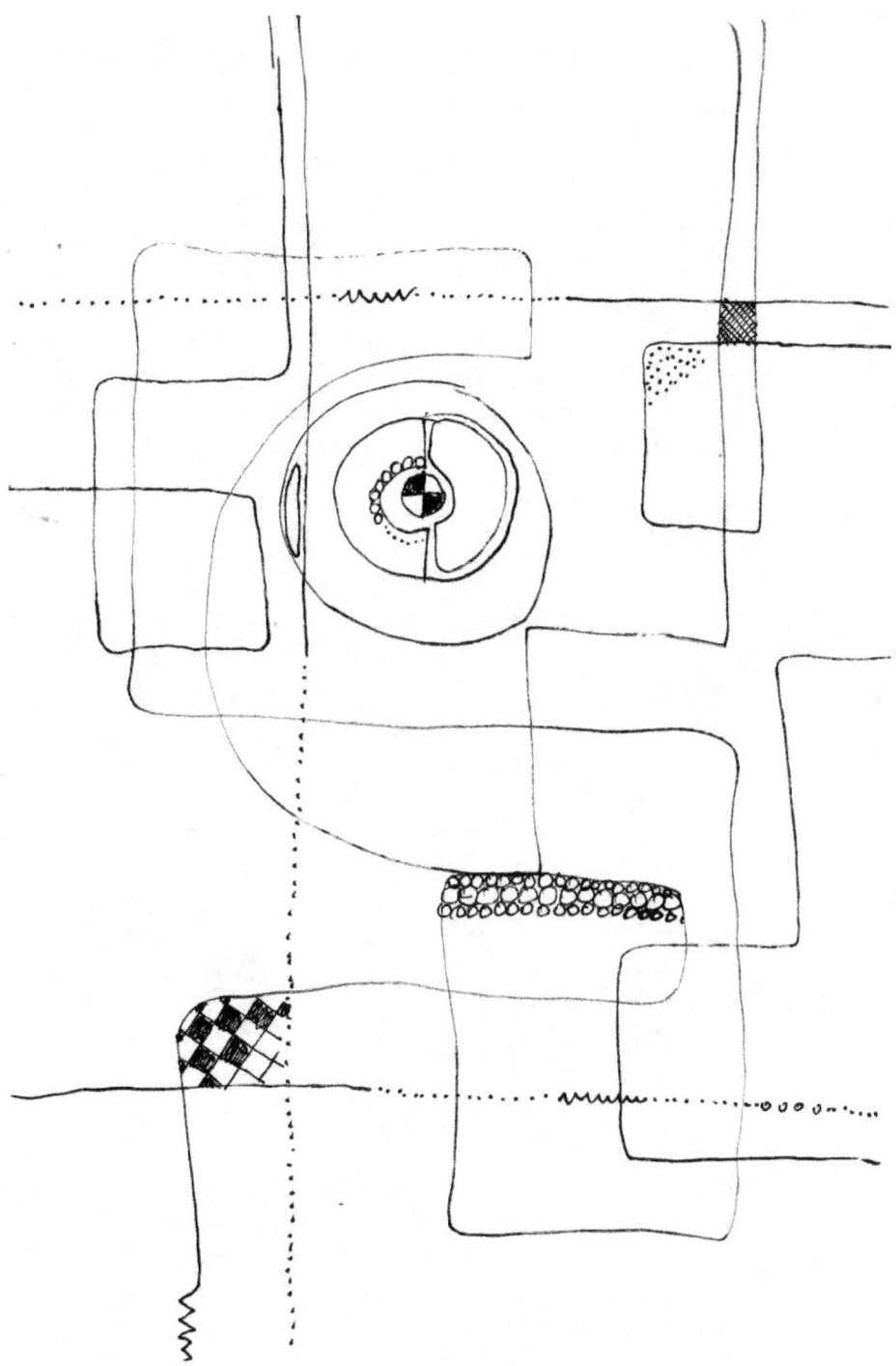

In the following pages, complete drawings, filling sections with different repetitive patterns, some sections leave blank. This is the intuitive drawing; use your imagination and feeling of harmony. Create, meditate, enjoy the process!

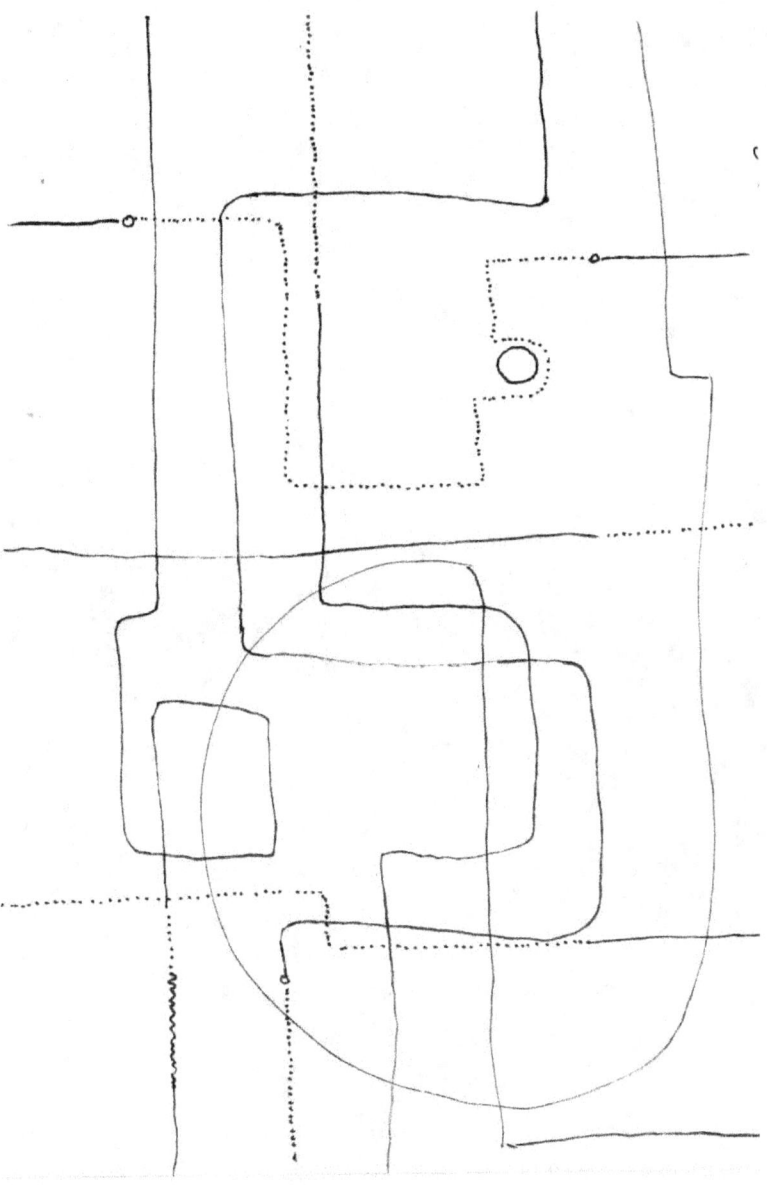

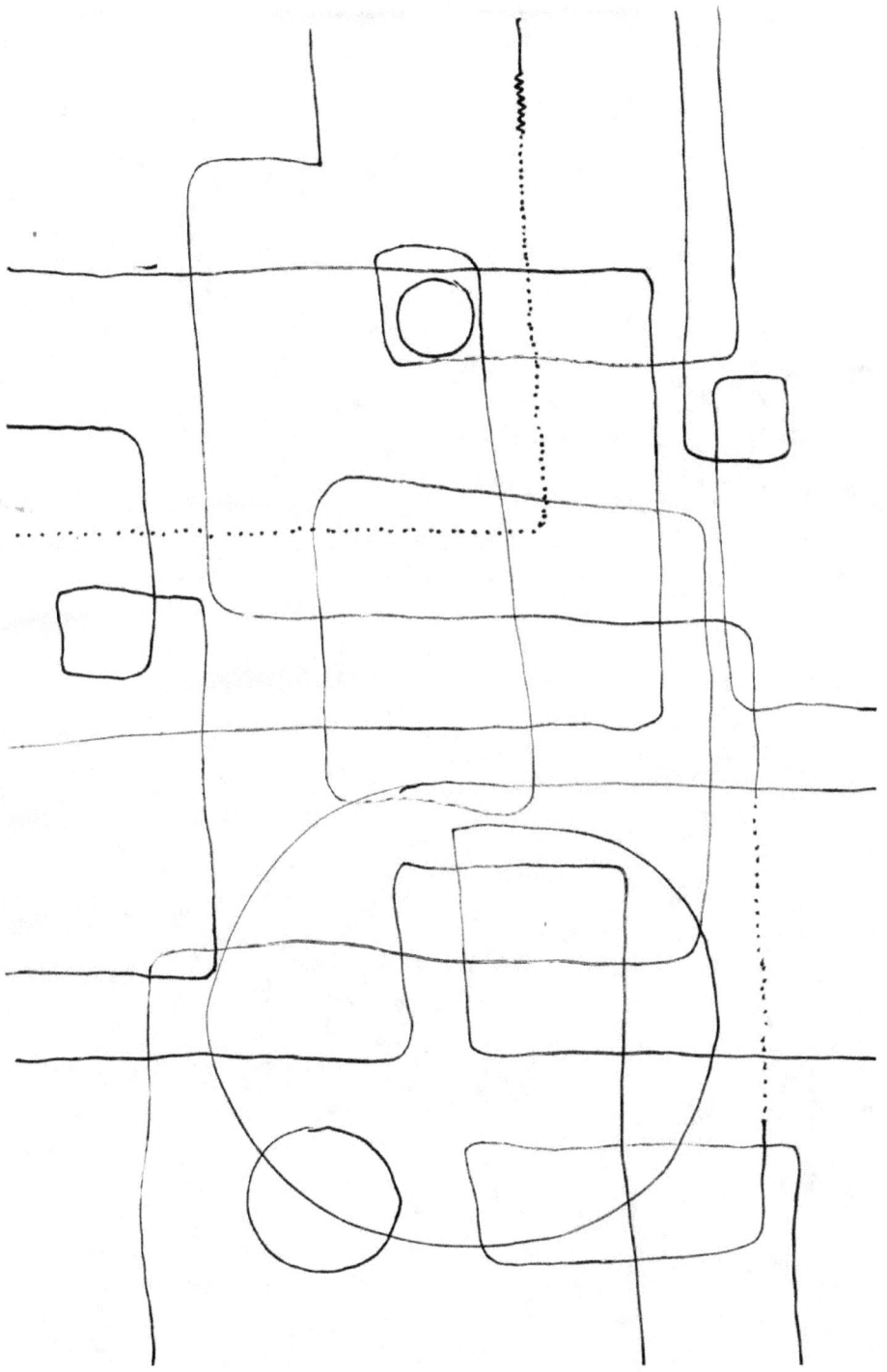

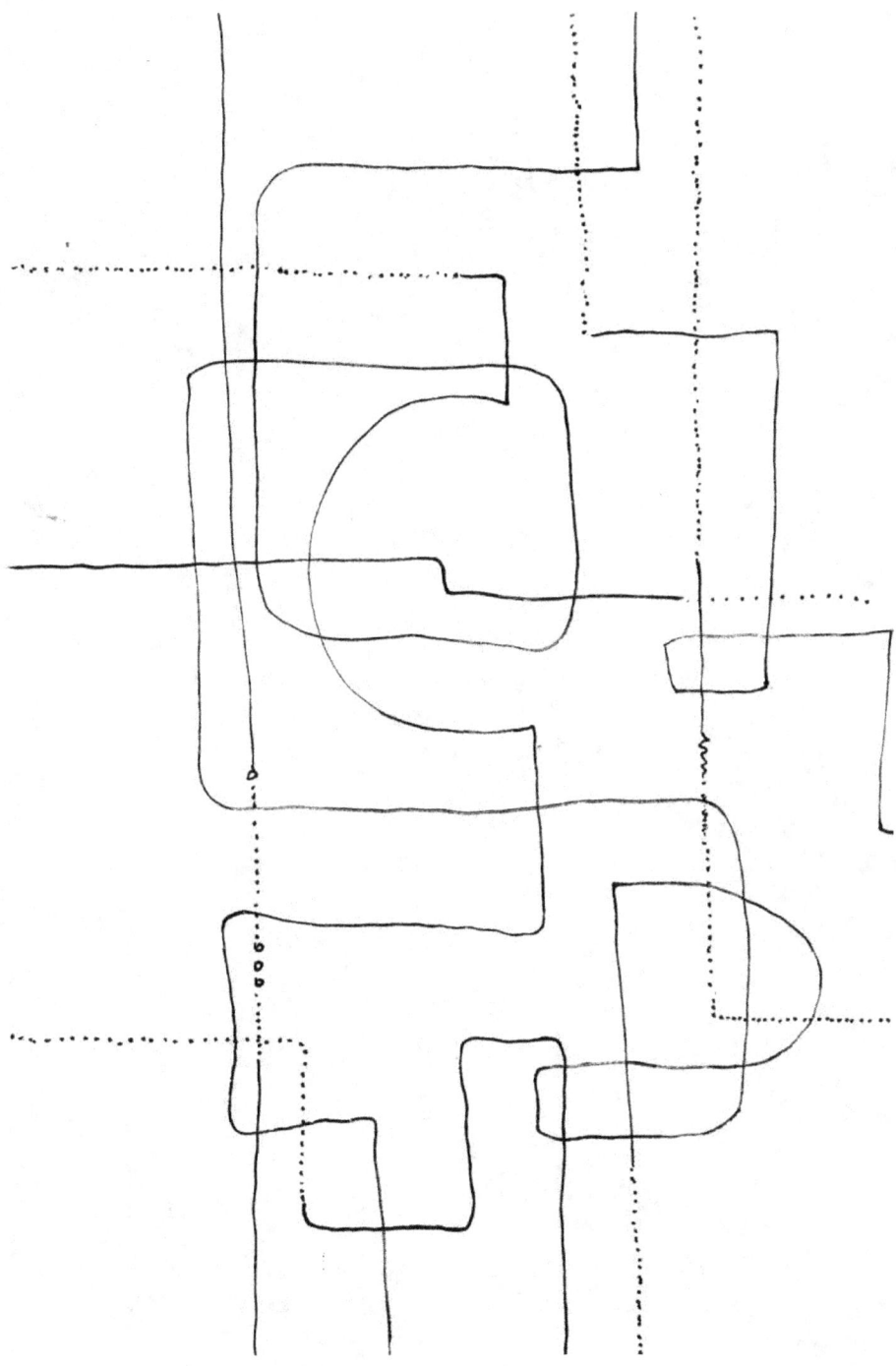

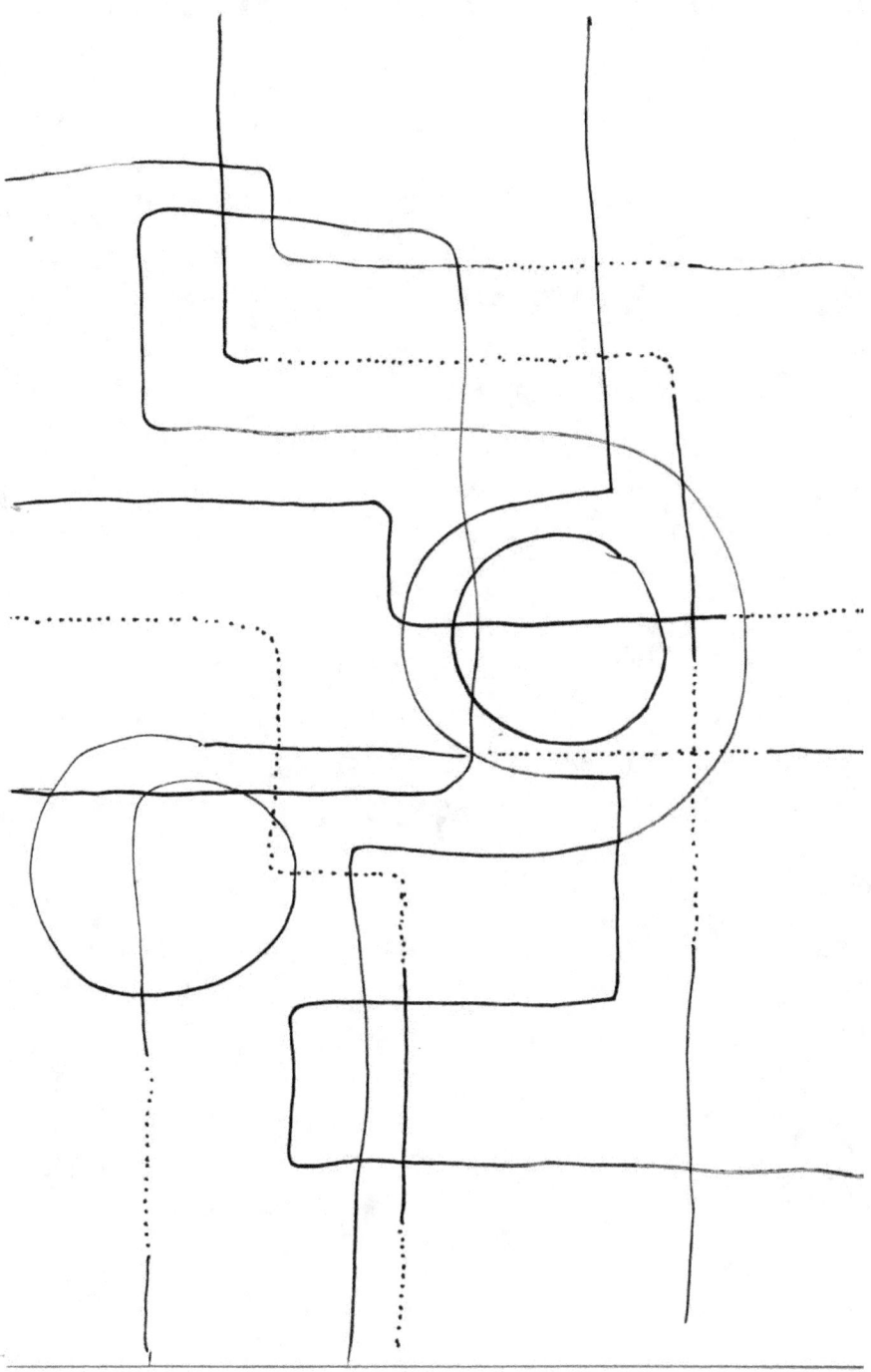

Create your repetitive patterns Gallery

The following pages invite you to create your personal repetitive patterns' Gallery here and now. All you need is a thin ink pen. Fill each section with different repetitive pattern. Use your imagination, make different combinations and variations of the line, circles, squares, dots, triangles, ovals, zigzags; twist and turn your line, follow your creative instinct. You will need these patterns' Gallery later, when you will draw your future images.

1	2	3
4	5	6

7	8	9
10	11	12
13	14	15
16	17	18

19	20	21
22	23	24
25	26	27
28	29	30

31	32	33
34	35	36
37	38	39
40	41	42

43	44	45
46	47	48
49	50	51
52	53	54

Create your abstract drawings from the scratch

The following pages (73-80) are for you to create your NeoPopRealist advanced abstracts drawings from the scratch. A few abstracts by Nadia Russ (pages 68-72) are here to give you some ideas about the variations. You should not copy them, they are copyrighted; create new abstracts. Always use ink pen. Do not worry if you make a "mistake" or two. Do not try to erase them; they will disappear with new repetitive patterns that will balance the whole composition. Open your mind, impossible is nothing, draw your images with ease. The repetitive patterns' drawing process will open you doors to the level of meditation and relaxation you never experienced before, purifying your mind. And as a result, you will discover new you, with wide eyes open to new opportunities in arts and life.

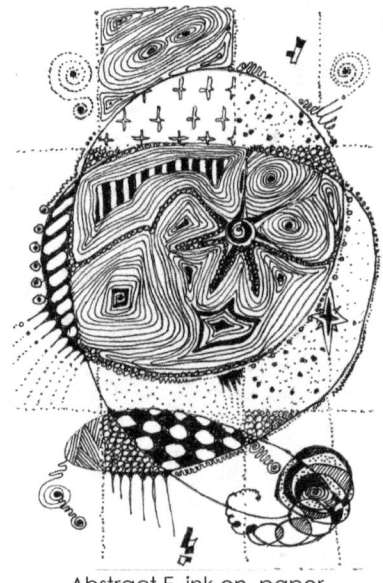

Abstract E, ink on paper

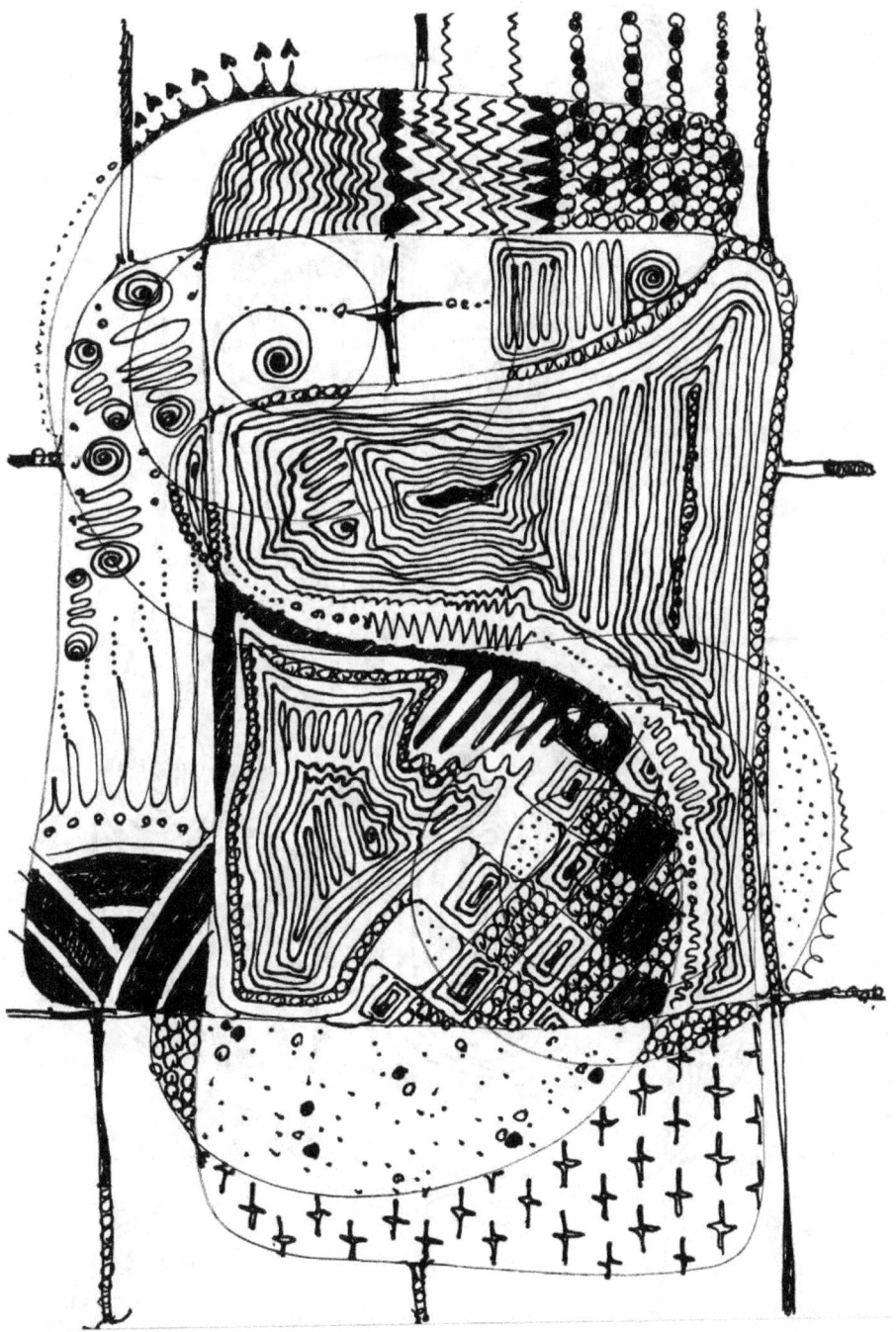

Abstract F, ink on paper

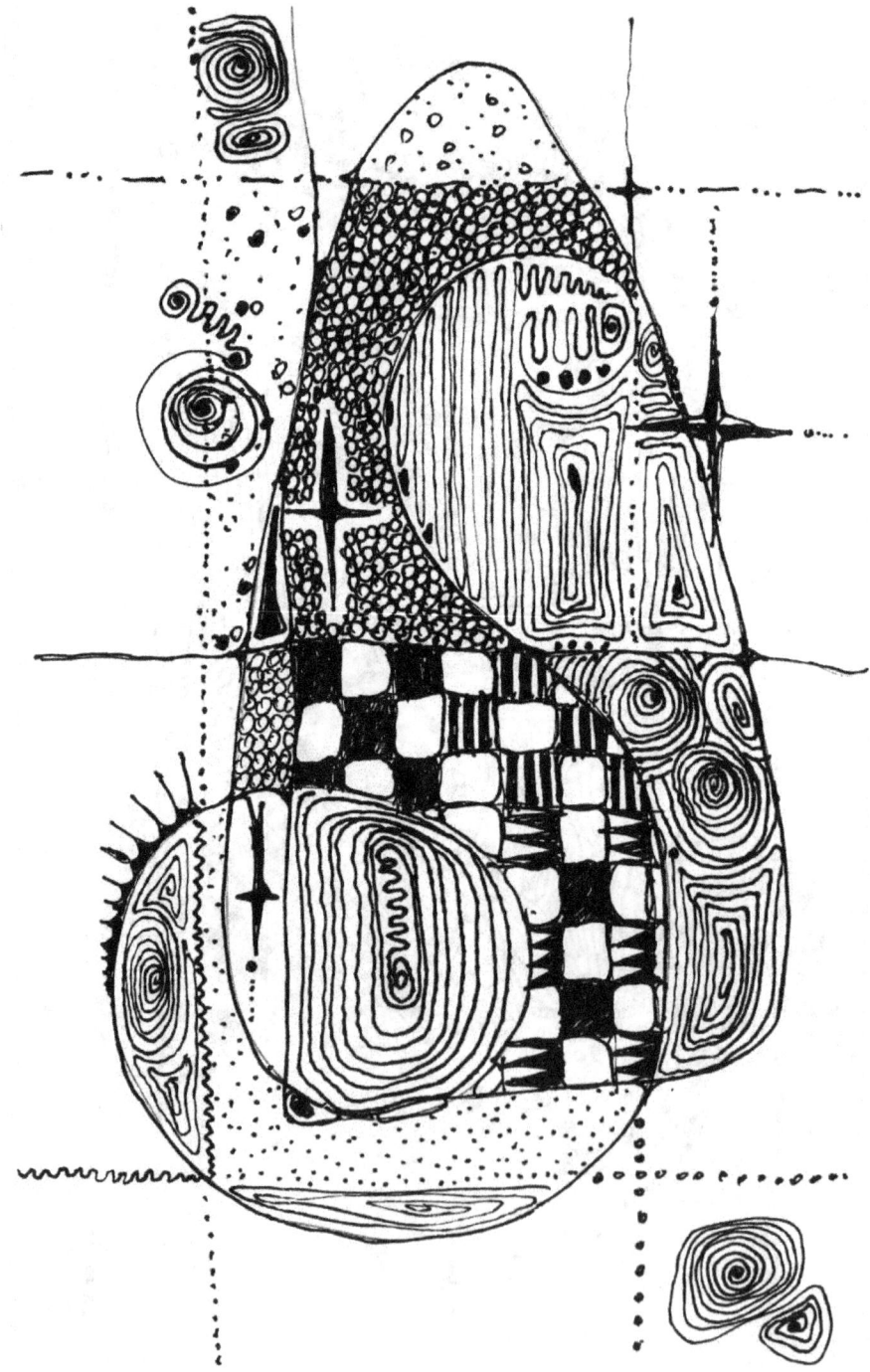

Abstract G, ink on paper

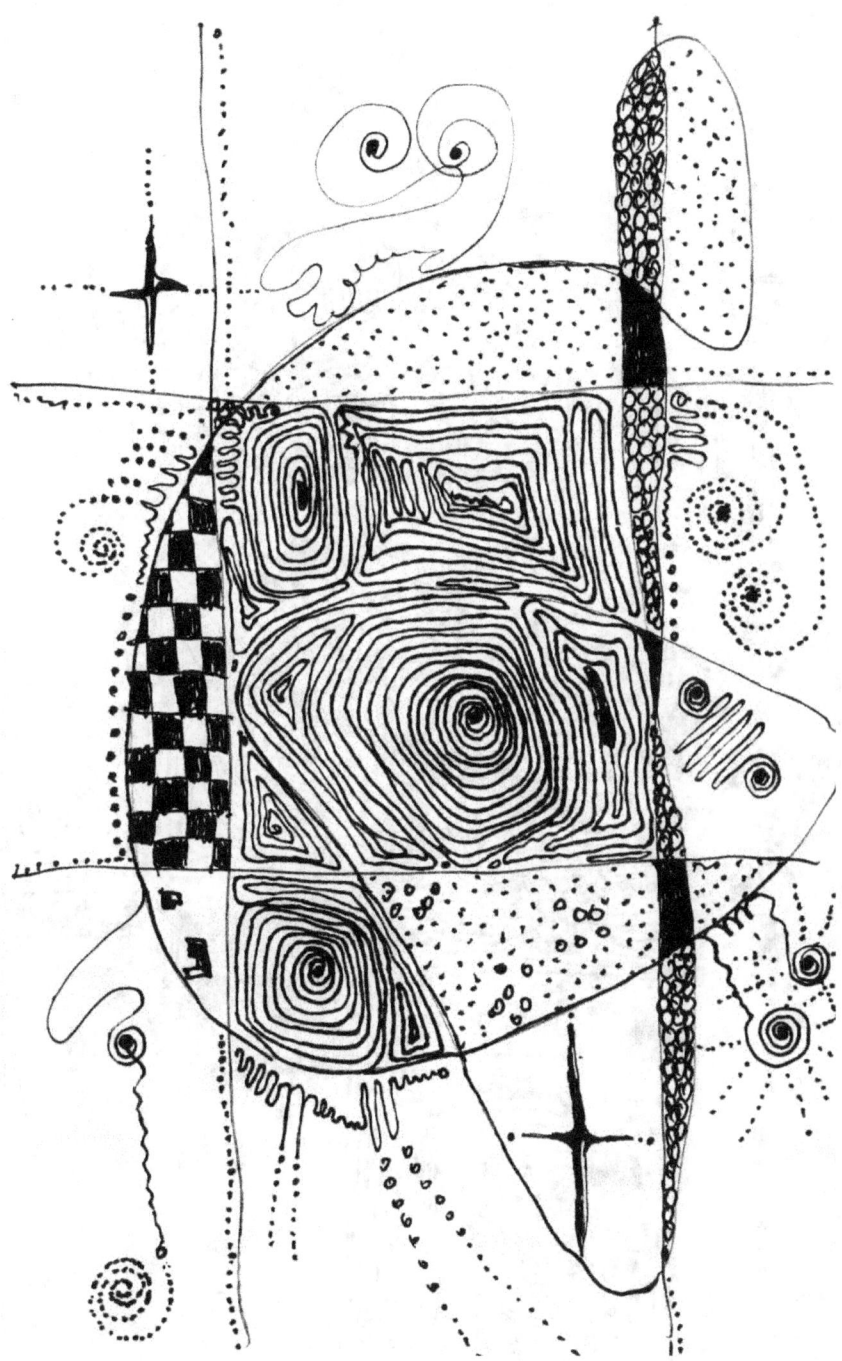

Abstract H, ink on paper

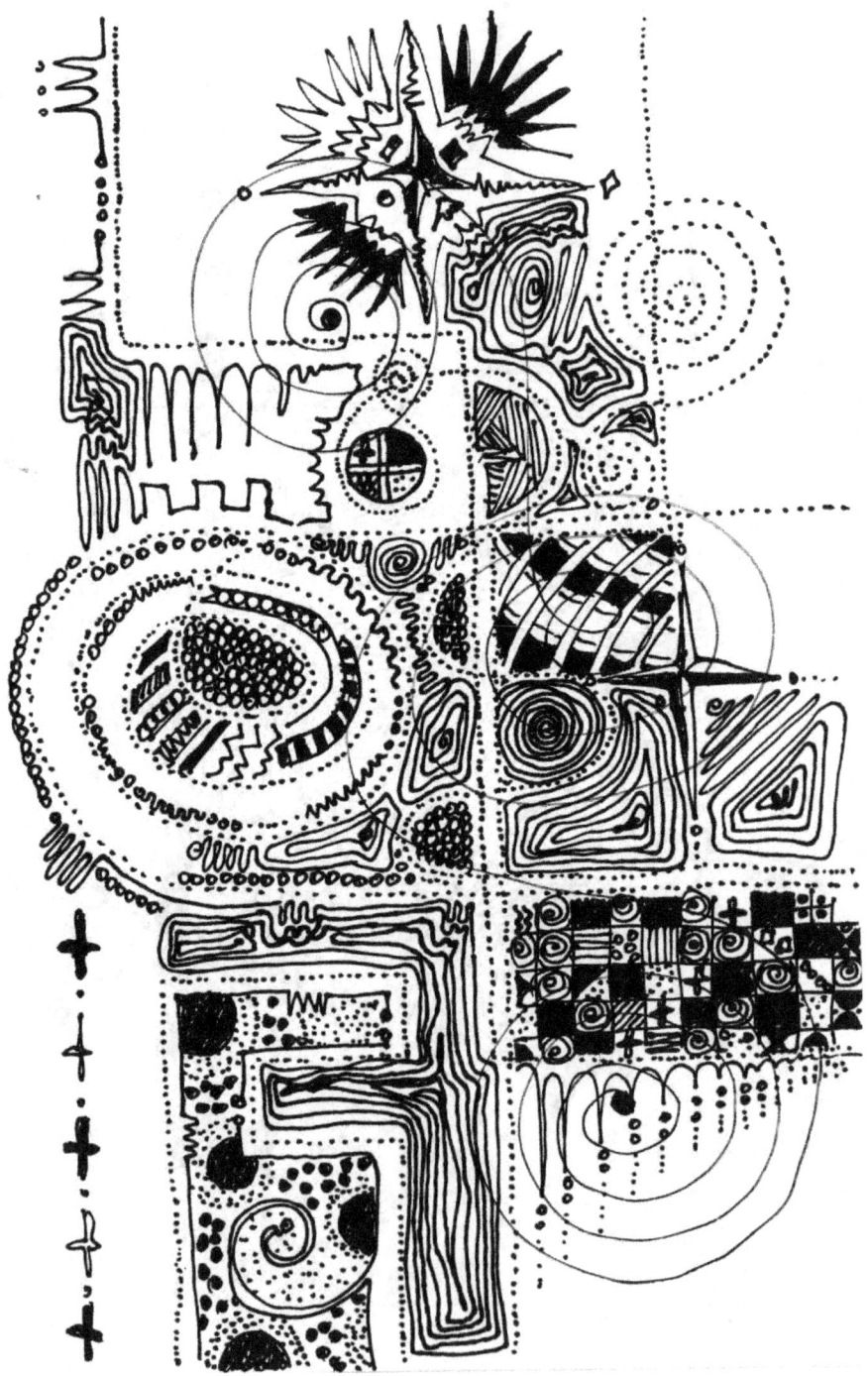

Abstract J, ink on paper

About NeoPopRealism creator

NADIA RUSS

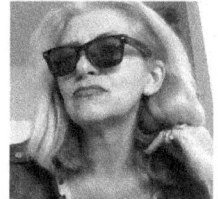

Nadia Russ (aka Nadejda Maloletneva) was born into a former professional military officer's family. As a child, she began studying art from famous masters of the past through art books and reproductions, which her mother Vera was collecting in their home. Nadia daily heard about and saw the reproductions of works of Leonardo da Vinci, Michelangelo, Rafael, contemporary Russian artists such as Petrov-Vodkin.

She began painting and drawing seriously in 1989. A few months later, her first ink drawings were exhibited in a group exhibition in famous Moscow's Manege and later, in other Moscow's art galleries. In 1992, she successfully showed her work in New York City.

In 1996-2000, Nadia resided in the Bahamas, where her work gained some special brightness. There, she got her pseudonym to her original 'Nadejda Maloletneva', which was easier to pronounce - 'Nadia Russ'. In 2000-2001, in Xanadu hotel, she operated her Art Gallery Club 13.

In 2000, she moved to the United States, where she lives up until present. January 4, 2003, Nadia Russ created a word NeoPopRealism and manifested internationally new style of visual arts which combines the brightness and simplicity of Pop Art with deep and psychological realism and has graphic nature. Her artworks are in private and permanent public collections including MOYA - Museum of Young Art in Vienna (Austria), Simferopol and Sumy Art Museums in Ukraine, Kinsey Institute of Indiana University (USA), Ukrainian Museum in New York City (USA), WEAM - World Erotic Art Museum in Miami (USA), Schacknow Museum of Fine Arts (USA), Historical Museum of Fort Lauderdale (USA), Lebedyn and Konotop Art Museums (Ukraine), D. Burliuk Foundation (Ukraine), and other.

In 2008-2010, Nadia Russ founded and juried Int'l NeoPopRealism Starz Art competitions. In 2009-2011, she authored a few art-related books such as "NeoPopRealism Starz: 21st Century ART" two volumes, "New Millennium ART", "Fort Lauderdale 100: A Must-Have Collector's Edition" three volumes, and a series of teaching/ leaning books on how to draw NeoPopRealism ink images. She is the founder (2007) of *NeoPopRealism Journal & Wonderpedia*, publications online, dedicated to arts, culture, books, news, celebrities and more. Nadia Russ lives in New York City and Florida. Visit her website at www.nadiaruss.com.

Conclusion

W hat is Art?

Now, when you learned how to draw the NeoPopRealism advanced abstract images, you might have your answer to this open question. We'll be happy to hear from you, e-mail us to neopoprealismpress@mail.com. Also, if you have a blog, post there images of your NeoPopRealism ink drawings. Have a wonderful journey to the world of NeoPopRealism!

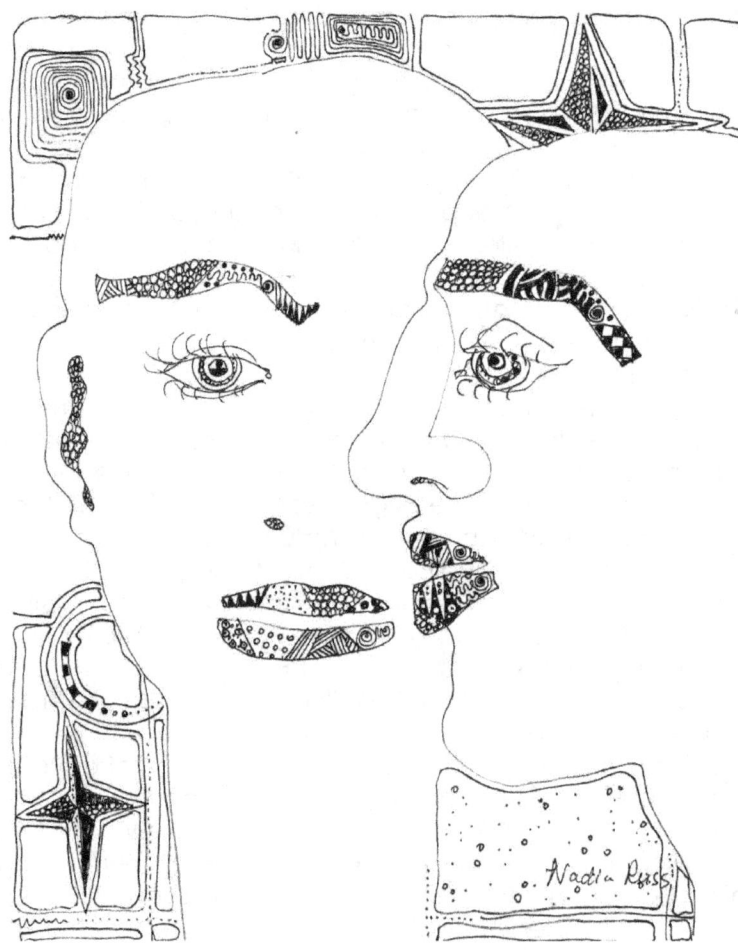

Nadia Russ, *People*, 8.5"x11", ink on paper, 2012

NeoPopRealism ten canons for happier life

1. Be beautiful.
2. Be creative and productive; never stop studying and learning.
3. Be peace-loving, positive-minded.
4. Do not accept communist philosophy.
5. Be free-minded, do the best you can to move the world to peace and harmony.
6. Be family oriented, self-disciplined.
7. Be free spirited. Follow your dreams, if they are not destructive, but constructive.
8. Believe in god. god is one. It is Harmony and striving for perfection.
9. Be supportive to those who need you, be generous.
10. Create your life as a great adventurous story.

Created by Nadia Russ in 2004

Additional books - teaching / learning material on NeoPopRealism Ink drawing for adults, teenagers and children

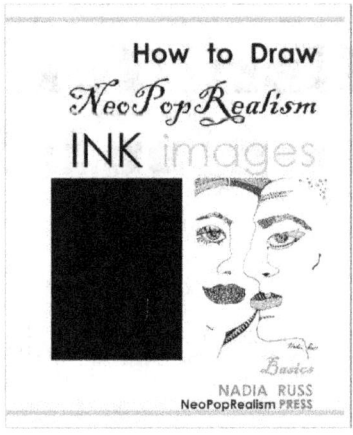

ISBN: 9780615515755
FOR TEENS & ADULTS

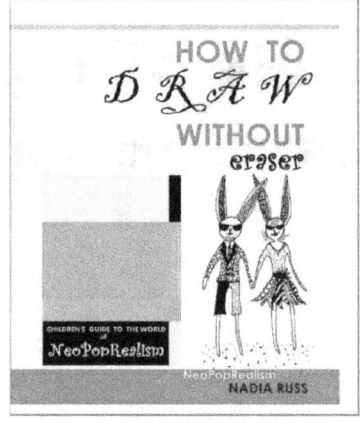

ISBN: 9780615521824
FOR CHILDREN

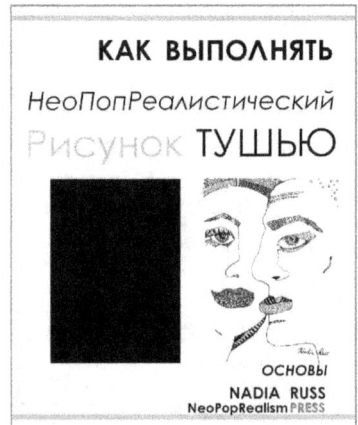

Book "*How to Draw NeoPopRealism Ink Images: Basics*" in Russian translation.
ISBN: 9780615516967

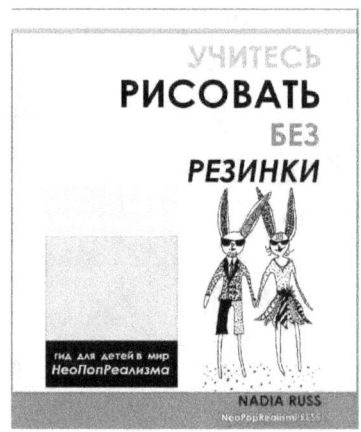

Book "*How to Draw Without Eraser: Backgrounds*" in Russian translation.
ISBN: 9780615523484

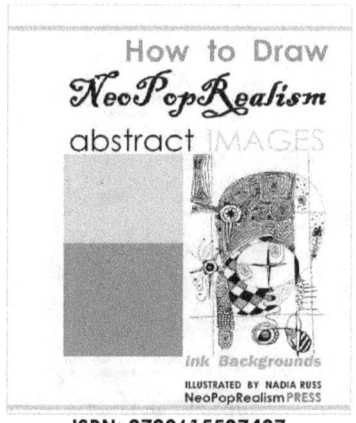

ISBN: 9780615527437
FOR TEENS & ADULTS

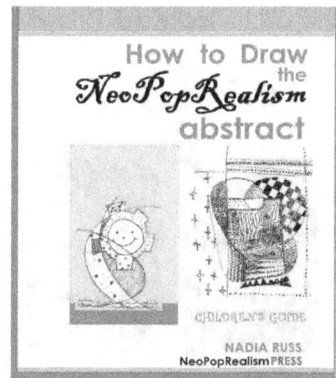

ISBN: 9780615545332
FOR CHILDREN

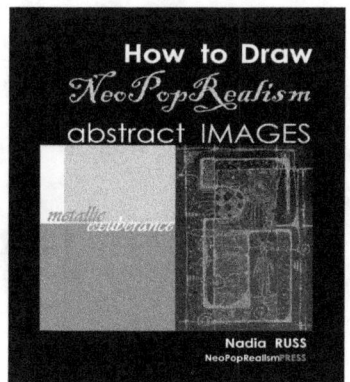

ISBN: 9780615560991
FOR TEENS AND ADULTS

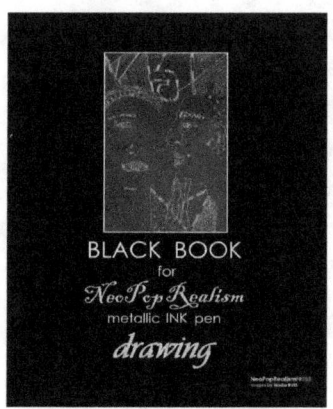

ISBN: 9780615561028
FOR TEENS AND ADULTS

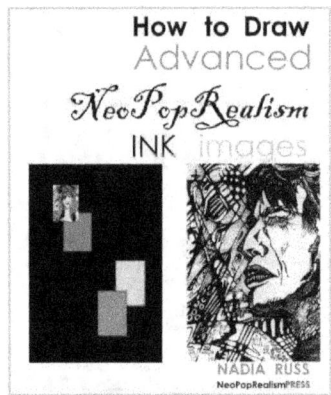

ISBN: 9780615569758
FOR TEENS AND ADULTS

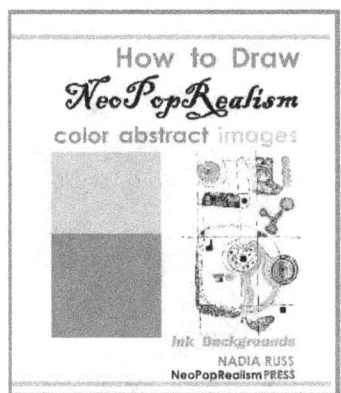

ISBN: 9780615579559
FOR TEENS AND ADULTS